The Mazinaw Experience

The Mazinaw Experience
Bon Echo and Beyond

JOHN CAMPBELL

NATURAL HERITAGE BOOKS

The Mazinaw Experience
Bon Echo and Beyond
John Campbell
Natural Heritage/Natural History Inc.
Copyright © 2000 by John Campbell

Published by Natural Heritage/Natural History Inc.
(P.O. Box 95, Station O, Toronto, Ontario, M4A 2MB)

Designed by Gringo Design
Edited by Jane Gibson
Printed and bound in Canada by Hignell Book Printing, Winnipeg, Manitoba

"Untitled" in *Mazinaw*. Permission to use from author, Stuart McKinnon
Cover photograph: Ministry of Natural Resources
Back cover photographs: top, Courtesy Lennox and Addington County Museum, bottom, Courtesy Ministry of Natural Resource
Title page photograph by John Campbell

Any errors or omissions brought to the attention of the publisher will be corrected in subsequent editions.

Canadian Cataloguing in Publication Data

Campbell, John (John David Elliott)
   The Mazinaw experience : Bon Echo and beyond

Includes bibliographical references and index.
ISBN 1-896219-50-0

1. Bon Echo Provincial Park (Ont.) 2. Bon Echo Provincial Park (Ont.) –
History. 3. Natural history – Ontario – Bon Echo Provincial Park. 4.
Ontario, Eastern, – History, Local. I. Title.

FC306.B64C35 2000   971.3   C00-931218-8
F1059.B64C35 2000

THE CANADA COUNCIL | LE CONSEIL DES ARTS
FOR THE ARTS | DU CANADA
SINCE 1957 | DEPUIS 1957

Natural Heritage/Natural History Inc. acknowledges the support received for its publishing program from the Canada Council Block Grant Program and the assistance of the Association for the Export of Canadian Books, Ottawa. Natural Heritage also acknowledges the support of The Ontario Council for the Arts for its publishing program.

To my mother, Eva P. Campbell

Contents

Acknowledgements

One of the real pleasures in writing this book has been the encouragement and assistance received along the way. While the list of those who provided information and expressed support was long, there are a few who I would like to specifically mention: the Friends of Bon Echo Park, its President Betty Pearce, and their publication committee headed by Stuart MacKinnon, for their encouragement and suggestions; the staff of the Bon Echo Provincial Park, particularly Gary Sharman, Denice Wilkins and David Bree for generously allowing me access to their files and research. Evan Morton of the Heritage Centre in Tweed and The Pioneer Club in Cloyne allowed me access to their historical materials. It was also the original members of the Pioneer Club who produced the wonderful local history *The Oxen and The Axe* on which I relied. Bernice Wise, Elsie Snider and Ted Snider, whose families were pioneers in the area, confirmed a number of facts. Marg Axford and Ian Brumell also provided insights, particularly on the history of the upper lake. Olive Hall provided information on the Camp Mazinaw. The *Tweed News* and the *Napanee Beaver* permitted me to quote liberally from their articles of an earlier time and Janet Black was most generous in providing professional library research support. Ellen Reid toiled over early editing, providing valuable suggestions. A number of the present day photographs were shot by Astrid Fernandez and Lorna Seaman as well as David Bree and other staff of the Ministry of Natural Resources. I would also like to thank my publishers, Barry Penhale and Jane Gibson of Natural Heritage Books, Jane for her professional editorial assistance and Barry for his long-standing interest in the area and for having enough faith in this project to take the risk required.

But most of all, I would like to thank my parents and grandparents who, fifty years ago, joined with those who, over the years, have provided their families with the privilege of sharing in the Mazinaw experience.

John Campbell

Introduction

The original motivation for this publication came from a desire to know better a lake that I, and so many others, hold to be special. Little did I realize that the experience would be so enjoyable and the story so interesting.

The present day geology and topography of the region are the result of massive change over billions of years. These changes were influenced by a combination of many forces which include the rising and wearing away of ancient mountain chains, violent volcanic activity, tremendous titanic forces deep within the earth's crust and the repeated advance and retreat of massive glaciers. What has resulted ultimately is a place of natural beauty, which includes in its spectacular landscape a 107 metre, about 350 feet, of sheer cliff dropping into one of the province's deepest lakes.

The first presence of human life on the shores of the Mazinaw occurred well before the birth of Christ. These people, nomadic Algonkian hunters and gatherers, lived in a world heavily influenced by forces of nature largely beyond their control. They were drawn to this cliff as a sacred place where the spirits (Manitous) might speak to them in dreams and where, through rituals and prayer, the Algonkian might win their favour.

Although there is evidence of early contact with the French fur traders around 1670, the area remained relatively untouched until the 1850s, and was one of the last regions in Southern Ontario to be settled. It was the great forests filled with pines growing up to 38 metres or 125 feet in height, which attracted lumbering interests. The forest floor, carpeted by centuries of pine needles, was shaded by a canopy of branches so dense that only the odd shaft of light could penetrate. However, in this cathedral-like setting, the space between the trees was such that a lumber wagon could be driven between them without need of a trail. The days of lumbering are often typified as an era of great energy, ruggedness and adventure, but they were also an example of the mishandling of a valuable natural resource, occuring at a time when society's belief was that nature should be conquered and exploited rather than conserved and properly managed.

With the lumbering came the building of the Addington Colonization Road. Free land grants attracted settlers who hacked out clearings in the wilderness and built log cabins. Their experience was one of early struggle as they built their meagre farms and created local communities. Fortunately for them, the lumber companies provided winter employment and a ready market for produce. After the last of the pine had been harvested, however, the logging firms moved out, leaving the farmers stranded, distant from markets which could be reached only over the poorest of roads. A series of fires, burning the thin glacial soil down to the bedrock, added to the difficulties of survival, and to the ultimate demise of agriculture in the area.

Although destroyed by fire over 65 years ago, the legacy of the Bon Echo Inn is still very much alive in the form of the lake's provincial park. The history of the hotel started with its creation as a high risk venture by a young nature enthusiast named Weston Price, who eventually would become renowned as a pioneer in American dentistry. Ten years later, the inn would be purchased by Flora MacDonald Denison, a spiritualist and first president of Canada's suffragette movement, the Dominion Women's Enfranchisement Association. She turned the hotel into a haven for those interested in the arts. Upon her death, the hotel's management was passed to her son, Merrill Denison, one of Canada's first playwrights. Guests over the years included members of the Group of Seven, Yousef Karsh, James Thurber, Horace Traubel and W.O. Mitchell. As well as being a celebrated author, Merrill was an ardent conservationist and spokesperson for a greater understanding of the hardships faced by the farmer of the Canadian Shield – a position that reflected his own Mazinaw experience.

Human existence in this area has always been an economic challenge. As Denison predicted, farming has been replaced by tourism, now the driving economic force for the area. People in the region continue to build on earlier struggles, maintaining local villages with a reputation for resourcefulness and resiliency.

This is also the story of a unique natural setting, a transition zone in which a Canadian Shield environment in Southern Ontario provides a home for both plants and animals usually found either farther to the south or to the north. While the great pine forests of yesterday will never return, today's mixture of coniferous and deciduous trees, combined with dry rocky barrens, peat bogs, rivers and lakes, offer habitat for a wide variety of mammals, amphibians, birds, fish and insects.

The towering landmark in the region is, of course, the Rock which gives the Provincial Park its name. Over the years much has been learned about Bon Echo's geological formation, its ecology and mythology. Although the ancient Algonkians were the first to have been touched by its majesty, they were certainly not the last.

If this publication helps others to see more clearly the ghosts of Mazinaw's past, the complexity and fragile nature of her present and the importance of protecting her future, it will more than have served its purpose.

FIRST NATIONS PERIOD

500 to 800 BC	Evidence of camps established on the lake during the Mid-Woodlands archaeological period
period up to 1600s	Algonkian territory – nomadic hunters and gathers
1650 to 1750	Iroquois invasion and control
1680 to 1725	Contact with French fur traders
1760 – 1800	Ojibwa/Mississauga/Algonkian – drive Iroquois further south and intermarry with captives
early 1800s	Indigenous peoples in area relocated to reserves near Peterborough
1850s	Logging and settlement begins

CHAPTER I

First Nations Period

The very name "Mazinaw" reflects its Native heritage. Until the 1930s, the names Mazinaw, Mishinog and Massanoga, were used interchangeably and were believed to mean "a place of meeting." The book *The Oxen And The Axe* has an alternate definition of the word "Mazinaw," meaning "picture or painting," taken from the Algonkian, "Mu-zi-nu-ki-gum." According to this interpretation, the lake originally was named after the pictographs which appear on the Rock's surface just above the waterline. To add to the confusion, there are up to nine different spellings of the Native word for picture, writing or painting.[1]

The Aboriginal experience in the Mazinaw area is part of a much broader history. At the dawn of the fur trade in the early 1600s, there were two distinct linguistic Native groups in the Eastern Great Lakes and St. Lawrence regions, the Algonkian and Iroquois confederacies. The Algonkian linguistic group consisting of the Algonkian, Ottawa, Cree and Ojibwa tribes, controlled the land north of the St. Lawrence up into the Ottawa Valley and across to Georgian Bay, as well as the mountainous territory south of Montreal in what is now modern day New York State. The

Iroquoian Confederacy was composed of the Mohawk, Oneida, Onondaga, Cayuga and Seneca and was located both north and south of Lake Ontario, the Mohawks being located closest to the Mazinaw region. Years earlier the Huron had also roamed Eastern Ontario, but gradually had moved north and west to congregate around Lake Simcoe in the area commonly called Huronia, attracted there by the easily cultivated sandy soils and by the good fishing and transportation provided by Georgian Bay.

Until the early 1600s, the Mazinaw region was the preserve of the Algonkian. A hunting and gathering society, they moved in family groupings of 25 to 50 people as the presence of game and suitable plant life dictated. Although wandering widely, they revisited the same sites on a seasonal or periodic basis, their customs and technology reflecting this nomadic existence. Shelter was provided by wigwams covered in birchbark, skins or woven mats of reed. In summer, they traversed the lakes and rivers in birchbark canoes, and moved over the land following well-travelled paths. Clothing was mostly of deerskin with other animal fur added in the winter. The bow and arrow were important tools for hunting; bows were made of oak, or ash and measured approximately four feet long. Arrows were often cut from the stalks of the Juneberry bush. Meat from small game or deer was boiled, or roasted and eaten immediately after the kill, or cut in strips and dried over a smoky flames to be stored for later use.

According to the records left by the Jesuit fathers, the early explorers and fur traders, such as La Salle, the Aboriginals of the Canadian Shield were a hardy breed. Largely free of disease, they could keep on the trail almost day and night with little food or sleep, sometimes for ten days at a stretch.

In the first decade of the 1600s, the Algonkians controlled traffic along the St. Lawrence River. When Samuel de Champlain founded the city of Quebec in 1608 by building a trading post there, the Algonkians tried to enforce a monopoly on trade with the French, excluding the Iroquois and acting as middlemen with the Huron. The Iroquois, recognizing the growing value of furs for trade with the English, started attacking the French trade routes, stealing the furs and killing those with whom they came in contact. In response, the Algonkians sought out the Hurons and the French as allies in defense against this challenge.

In 1615, Champlain joined an expedition of Hurons and Algonkians. The purpose of the trip was to survey hunting grounds in Eastern Ontario and to attack any Iroquois encountered. On the return leg of this foray, the party passed through the area just to the south of the Mazinaw and camped for a number of days to rest and replenish their food supplies. While there, Champlain recorded his observations on the Aboriginal use of a deer trap to catch game:

> *The enclosure was made by a stockade eight or nine feet high and about 1,500 paces long on each side. At the apex of this triangle, there was a little yard which grew narrower and narrower, covered in part by branches leaving an opening of only five feet . . . by which the deer were to enter. . . . When everything was ready, they started half an hour before daylight to go into the wilderness about half a league from their enclosure, separated from each other 80 paces, each having two sticks which they beat together, marching slowly in this order until they came to their enclosure. When the deer heard this noise, they fled before them until they reach the enclosure onto which the savages drive them and gradually they come together at the opening of their triangle. Here the deer move along the sides of the stockade until they reach the end, towards which the savages pursue them sharply with bow and arrows in hand, ready to shoot.*[2]

The Mohawks/Iroquois, while recognized as warriors, were in many ways a more advanced society than the nomadic Algonkian. As the lands they occupied were generally more suited to agriculture, more permanent settlements were possible. They lived in long-houses, wooden structures which accommodated large extended family groupings and were organized into villages surrounded by picket palisades. Over time they developed agricultural implements, thus enabling more extensive cultivation of maize and other grains in fields which stretched, in some cases, for great distances beyond their settlements.

As interest in the fur trade grew, the value of furs increased and disputes over hunting territories intensified. In 1616, the Iroquois mounted a large and sustained invasion into the land of the Algonkian. These warriors were armed with rifles, steel hatchets and knives which they had purchased at the Dutch and English settlements in, what is now, Upper New York State. The invasion was so successful that, by 1640, they had almost eradicated the Huron and had expelled the Algonkian. From 1650 to 1750, the Mazinaw area, as well as all of Southeastern and Central Ontario, became known as the hunting ground of the Iroquois.

The Algonkian, faced with this overwhelming threat, retreated into Northwestern Ontario and Quebec. There they remained for over a century, leaving Southeastern Ontario, including the Mazinaw area, sparsely populated. By the early 1700s, however, the population of the Iroquois declined, a result of diseases introduced by the Europeans. They now were forced to strike a more neutral stance, in the face of the strong military presence of both the French and English. Finally, around 1760, the Ojibwa and Algonkian, sensing the reduced strength of their old foe, reasserted themselves and drove the Iroquois back south to the Lake Ontario and St. Lawrence River area. This effort was led by the Mississauga (members of the Ojibwa tribe) who originally had settled in the area around Manitoulin Island, but whose influence was later to be felt throughout Southern Ontario.

There is a local legend of a battle with the Iroquois having taken place at the Narrows on the Mazinaw. Another legend describes a battle which was fought on the top of the Rock. The Iroquois were said to have been lured to the edge of the cliff, attacked from behind and to have fallen to their death. No archeological evidence exists, however, to support these tales. What is known, is that the Algonkian and Ojibwa were successful in obtaining control of the area. Often they intermarried with their captives and, by 1800, had completely taken over the territory.[3]

The sheer face of Bon Echo Rock. Courtesy John Campbell.

View of the Mazinaw from the top of the Rock.
Courtesy John Campbell.

The Ojibwa, like the Algonkian before them, were hunters and gatherers who fished and harvested plant roots, wild rice and berries. The women collected water lily seed pods and popped the seeds like corn or ground them into flour. They also made a wide variety of baskets and containers from cedar bark and from straight grass which grows in the bottom of streams. During the summer, the Ojibwa used dip nets and gill nets to catch fish. In the winter, they cut holes in the ice and used small carvings of minnows to attract fish to the holes where they would then be speared. They also were known for the production of maple syrup. Their process involved making a vertical slash about five centimetres (two inches) deep and two centimetres (an inch) long in a sugar maple tree; a flat stick was then driven into the trunk at the base of the slash. The sap ran down this stick and was collected in a birch bark trough. It was then boiled by dropping hot rocks into the trough. Both syrup and sugar were produced in this manner, with the first sugar of the spring being offered to the spirits for their kindness in protecting them over the winter months.

One of a number of Native artifacts found in the region. Courtesy Ministry of Natural Resources.

During the summer the Ojibwa congregated at the mouths of the rivers entering Lake Ontario where they subsisted on seasonal hunting and fishing along with the gathering of various berries, roots and wild rice. The winter found them wandering the interior forests, living off preserved foods and game such as deer, hare and porcupine. Eventually, treaties resulted in the resettlement of the Mississauga from this region to Alderville, a reserve in Northumberland County near Rice Lake.

While there is no indication of permanent Native settlements in the Mazinaw area, archaeologists have found evidence of seasonal camps at both the tip of the Narrows opposite Bon Echo and the beach just to the south. The first site dates from the Mid-Woodlands period which lasted from 500 BC to 800 AD, and contains remnants of old fire pits, stone implements and ceramics, as well as the bones of fish and animals. The second site is Algonkian/Ojibwa in origin. It contains objects of European manufacture, including three hand-wrought nails, a Jew's harp and two French gun flints. This second site dates from between 1680 and 1725, the period of the French fur trade in the area. Such artifacts also have been found at the head of the lake, on top of the Rock, in Tapping's Bay, just north of the Park, and in various locations throughout the surounding area, including the north shore of Shabomeka Lake. On the top of the Rock there is a boulder circle near the main lookout, which may have been man-made, possibly the site of Native ceremonies.

From other Mid-Woodland sites in Southern Ontario, it has been learned that an active trade between Native bands occurred over surprising distances. Evidence includes copper from Lake Superior, shells from Manitoba, obsidian from Wyoming, ochre from the Sudbury basin and conch shells from Mexico.

Many of the Aboriginal trails in Eastern Ontario were used from generation to generation. One such pathway was the Skootamatta Trail, connecting the Bay of Quinte, via the Moira and Skootamatta rivers, to Skootamatta Lake. Another trail led from there to the lower end of Mazinaw, joining the lake at the small bay just north of where Smart's Marina is now located. There was also a trail from the north end of Mazinaw to Effingham Lake and on to Weslemkoon Lake, giving access to the Madawaska River system and, from there, to the west. This latter trail was described in some detail, in 1901, by Robert Ellis of the Geological Survey of Canada. The people living in this area at the turn of the century referred to a trail known as the Indian Run, which went from Kilpecker Creek, about one mile above the Mazinaw, over to Effingham Lake. This may have been the original Indian trail. With Mazinaw as its head-waters, the Mississippi River also provided access to the east, through a series of interconnected lakes, all the way to the Ottawa River.

Because the Mazinaw was a lake which connected several river and trail systems, it is assumed it was known to a number of nomadic bands and used as a temporary camping and hunting site over thousands of years. In keeping with this Native heritage, a number of local lakes are now known by their Ojibwa/Algonkian names: Skootamatta (Loon Lake) – "the Trail to Big Open Water;" Kishkebus (Dyer Lake) – "Sawn Through" or "Cut Through;" Shabomeka (Buck Lake) – "Middle." Because there are no major river systems in the immediate area, the Mazinaw never became a significant centre of activity. The larger river systems in Southern Ontario, including the Ottawa, Madawaska, French, Trent/Severn, Humber, Niagara and Grand were all much more active.

The Mazinaw is located in what was a border territory between the Ojibwa/Algonkian and Mohawk/Iroquois where territorial control often changed hands. The people on the Tyendinaga Indian Reserve near Deseronto, only 64 kilometres (40 miles) to the south, are Mohawk. There are also accounts of a few Mohawk having lived at the south end of the Mazinaw in the early days of settlement. They were said to have driven the deer from Skootamatta over to the Mazinaw, and to have used a brush fence, much like the one described by Champlain, to corral the deer for slaughter close to the lake.

These people may have been members of the Bey family who lived on the point, just north of where Smart's Marina is now on the lower lake. Originally, they had come from further to the south and east of the area. The Beys were a most interesting family. Johnny Bey could turn his hand to any number of things. He built beautiful birch bark canoes and was quite a fiddle player. He is best known, however, as the discoverer of the most successful gold mine in the area, the Ore Chimney Mine which was in production intermittently between 1909 and 1936. He and his wife Anna made baskets and other Native handcraft of excellent quality.

While little is known about the interaction of First Nations people with the Mazinaw, it is safe to assume that for centuries, small family bands of hunters and gatherers visited the lake in their seasonal sojourns, camping at the Narrows and fishing in her waters. We certainly are not the first to have camped by her shores or to have viewed the lake from the top of Bon Echo. We also know that the cliff was well-known to the Native population and played a pivotal role in their relationship with the lake. Today it is still regarded as a spiritual site.

PICTOGRAPHS AND MYTHOLOGY

pre 1600s	Aboriginal peoples create pictographs
1670s	Concept of mythological figure of Nanabush possibly influenced by first contact with French Jesuits
1848	J.S. Hargen, first white person known to have described the pictographs
1879	A.J.B. Halfpenny describes the pictographs in the *Canadian Antiquarian and Numismatic Journal*
1880s	Pictographs described in publications by Smithsonian Institute and Canadian Department of Indian Affairs
1892	David Boyle, from the newly created Royal Ontario Museum, first to formally study the pictographs
1958	Selwyn Dewdney and Kenneth Kidd do tracings of the pictographs
1977	Gail McKnight studies images by means of light sensitive photographs
1992 and 1994	Canadian Conservation Institute compiles photographic record of rock paintings

CHAPTER 2

Pictographs and Mythology

The religious beliefs of the Algonkian centred on the concept of Manitou, meaning spirit, energy or power. They believed that Manitou was in all things – animals, plants, wind, thunder, water and rocks. Kitchi-Manitou was the greatest spirit of all. He was the Creator of the universe and the one who had given people the power to dream. It was through dreams that man could find purpose and meaning in life.

The Algonkians were heavily dependent on nature; many of the factors which spelled success or disaster being beyond their control. Much of their spiritual life thus focused on establishing contact and winning favour with these elemental forces and, in so doing, to gain some security in what was often a harsh and cruel environment. As in numerous other Aboriginal societies, the shaman (spiritual leader) played an important role, acting as a key communication link between the real and spirit worlds. Certain unique natural places would be selected as vision sites. If a Manitou favoured a shaman with a dream vision at such a site, the shaman would draw the vision in red ochre on the rock. Today we call these images pictographs.[1]

Red ochre (hematite) was regarded as a powerful sacred substance and was an important ingredient in the shaman's medicine bag. It was believed that by using its power, the shaman could breath life into his drawings. This material was mined in the Sudbury area, as well as other sites in the province. The ochre was combined with water and heated, producing a bright red, magnetized paste which adhered to the rock. Because the water level of the lake was lower then, the artists would have had to stand in their canoes to do the painting. It is believed that they used their fingers to create images rather than a brush or other implement.[2]

Altogether, there are 295 pictographs located along the base of Bon Echo, the largest collection of such rock drawings in Ontario It is very difficult to date the pictographs accurately because no organic material was used in their formation, but some experts feel they are in the range of 300 years old and were painted by Ojibwa/Algonkian Indians. Evidence for this view includes the fact that the Rabbit Man (Nanabush or Nanabozko), one of the main spirits depicted on the Rock, while known to many Native peoples, was particularly revered by the Ojibwa. It is considered doubtful that the Iroquois were the artists since they used agricultural implements and liked to depict such tools in their drawings. No agricultural symbols appear at Mazinaw.

Other authorities feel the pictographs, because of their rudimentary nature, were painted by a much earlier people. In comparison, Ojibwa pictographs in other parts of Ontario (Peterborough and Lake Superior) are much clearer, more complex and less abstract in design. The state of weathering of this art, almost to the point of extinction, is also cited as possible evidence of an earlier origin.

Another possible explanation for their abstract nature suggests that they were created to represent the visions or dream quests which youth experienced as part of their rites of passage into adulthood. The Native people believed that lesser spirits, or Manitous, were associated with certain animals. Each person, during a period of religious fasting, would try to establish a relationship with one. Often the decision of which Manitou to choose as a spiritual guardian would be decided by a dream.

The pictographs are now badly faded. Weather, ice, acid rain and even the mild acid from fingers, all have had a corrosive effect. Frost has caused exfoliation, the falling away of small pieces of ochre. The many different species of lichen covering the rock also have eaten away at the images. Unfortunately, there is little that can be done to prevent further deterioration. Over the years, silica from groundwater has gradually formed a thin shellac-like layer over the images. While this layer does act as a preservative, it also further obscures their outline.

Over the years, the Mazinaw pictographs have been the subject of considerable study. In February 1848, J.S. Hargen was sent to survey the Mississippi River system and is the first known white person to have made a record of them. The pictographs also were described by A.J.B. Halfpenny in an 1879 edition of the *Canadian Antiquarian and Numismatic Journal* [3] and by personnel from both the Smithsonian Institute and the Canadian Department of Indian Affairs in the 1880s. David Boyle, Director of the Provincial Museum, forerunner of the Royal Ontario Museum, was the first to formally study the pictographs in 1892.

Some three-quarters of a century later, in 1958, Selwyn Dewdney made a record of the images by applying a wet sponge to Japanese rice paper to make it translucent, and then used chalk to outline the figures. With his partner Ken Kidd, the curator of ethnology at the ROM, he recorded the findings in their book, *Indian Rock Paintings Of The Great Lakes*. In 1977, Victor Pelsea and Gail McKnight, both archeological researchers, took light-sensitive photographs of the pictographs, projected them on to paper and using a red felt marker, filled in all spaces showing red ochre. In this way they were able to capture even those parts of the pictographs too faded for the human eye to see. They recorded 295 hand-painted images, on 65 different rock faces covering over a two kilometre, a little over a mile stretch of shoreline. In the early 1990s, the Canadian Conservation Institute in Ottawa started the task of photographically cataloging the pictographs. They are preserving images of the drawings on high resolution film, using computer assisted techniques to enhance their clarity. This work is still continuing. Grace Rajnovich, in her 1994 publication *Reading Rock Art*, remarks on the uniqueness of the Mazinaw pictographs and suggests, "Further research may show that the seemingly personalized signs were, in fact, readable by many people back in the old days."[4]

One of the paintings illustrates what appears to be a human being with large ears. This figure is commonly known as the "Rabbit Man" and is believed to be a depiction of the Algonkian mythological spirit, Nanabush (Nanabozko), the fourth son of Kitchi-Manitou, the great spirit. This spiritual figure was common to a number of the tribes of northeastern North America. The characteristics ascribed to Nanabush, however, varied in degree from area to area. To some, he was a trickster or a god of fate, giving man both good and bad luck in a haphazard manner. He also was seen as a spirit who revelled in the pleasures of the flesh, both gastronomical and sexual. While the Ojibwa/Algonquin recognized these characteristics in Nanabush, their interpretation was of a more Christ-like figure. It is not clear if this latter interpretation was developed after the Native people first came into contact with the French in approximately 1670. Among the Ojibwa, Nanabush was also referred to as Wey-zuh-kay-chahk, which was later corrupted to "Whiskey Jack" or "Canadian Jay" by the early European newcomers.

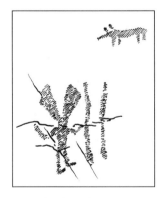 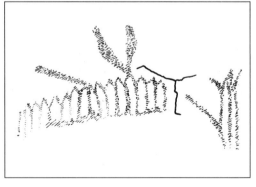

Nanabush and accompanying pictograph part of the Selwyn Dewdney collection of rice paper drawings at Mazinaw. Photograph courtesy of the Royal Ontario Museum, © ROM.

According to Algonkian beliefs, Kitchi-Manitou had a dream in which he envisioned Earth and all of its inhabitants. He set about to make the earth, with people being his last creation. To people he gave the power to dream. They had much to learn, however, and so Manitou took pity on them and assigned Nanabush to be their teacher. Nanabush was also to rule over nature. To assist him in his teaching role, he was given the power to turn himself into any natural form. His message was that man is to live with courage, strength, kindness, generosity and ingenuity. The Native people believed that Nanabush transformed himself into Bon Echo, as well as other special sites, as a way of teaching man how to live. Accordingly, they considered the Rock to be sacred.

There are many stories told about Nanabush. Like Aboriginal peoples everywhere, the Algonkian developed stories to explain how things had come to be as they are. The following are examples:

The Coming of Indian Summer

Long ago Nanabush and his brother Pee-Pauk-A Wis decided to have a race. Nanabush was far faster than his brother. Everywhere Nanabush's moccasins touched the earth, flowers sprang up and the land was at peace with the sky. Pee-Pauk-A-Wis was jealous and got angry. He punished the earth by making bad weather wherever his feet landed. Nanabush stopped at the Great Lakes to rest and fell asleep for the night. His brother overtook him and continued on north, creating bad weather. When Nanabush awoke, he realized what had happened and chased after his brother, creating Indian summer after the early fall cold. Whenever weather changed quickly, it was said that Nanabush and his brother were having a race.

Creation of the Milky Way

Nanabush called all of the animals together so that he could give them jobs to do: beavers to make dams; bees to make honey; woodpeckers to make forest music. All came and received jobs except the turtle. Turtle had been swimming under the water when Nanabush had called the animals. Instead of going to Nanabush to see what his duties were, he went down to the bottom of the lake and sulked. He stayed down there for a long time and got angrier and angrier. When finally he returned to the surface, he was so angry that, on seeing a canoe, he upset it and ate the surprised Ojibwa who were inside. The humans were very tasty and the turtle continued to attack canoes and eat people. On hearing of this, Nanabush suspected that turtle was angry at him and decided to make turtle do something useful. The next time that he saw turtle, he shot an arrow at him. Turtle dove into the water to escape the arrow. In doing so, he splashed the surface of the water with his tail, sending many water droplets up in a spray. Nanabush used his magic to hurl the droplets into the sky and to turn them into stars. These new stars formed the Milky Way.

How the White Birch Got Its Marks

The white birch tree has small black markings that look like miniature birds and pine needles. Legend has it that Nanabush became angry at the birch for falling asleep and allowing the birds to eat the meat outside of Nanabush's camp, which the birch was supposed to have been guarding. To punish the birch, and as a lesson to all that might disobey, he took a pine branch and whipped the birch. Pine sap rubbed off on its bark and some of the pine needles stuck to it. Nanabush then hurled the birds who had stolen his meat against the tree and some of them also stuck to the bark. As a reminder of this incident, all descendants of the birch now display these markings.

The Woodpecker's Red Crest

After his dinner had been stolen by wolves, Nanabush stopped into the camp of his friend, the giant woodpecker, for something to eat. The woodpecker decided that they would eat raccoon for dinner that evening. He took two long pieces of bone, stuck them in his nostrils and flew over to a tree and started to tap. In so doing, he shook a raccoon out of the tree and he and Nanabush had it for dinner. Nanabush wanted to return the favour and so invited woodpecker for dinner at his camp a little while later. When woodpecker arrived, Nanabush went outside, put two long pieces of wood in his nostrils and proceeded to climb a tree. He wanted to show wood-pecker that he could do the same trick. He started to peck at the tree. When the trick didn't work, he tapped harder. Woodpecker heard the noise and came running. He found Nanabush unconscious on the ground at the base of the tree, with blood running from his nostrils. Woodpecker propped Nanabush up against the base of the tree and stopped the bleeding. When Nanabush regained consciousness, woodpecker told him that he should never try that again and that how to tap on trees was a woodpecker secret. Nanabush was so grateful to woodpecker for saving his life that, as a reward, he gave him a red crown of feathers that all woodpeckers to this day display proudly. From that time on, the Native people used the red tufted woodpecker feathers to decorate their pipes.

How The Maple Trees Saved Nokomis

Nanabush's enemies, the Wendigoes, were always trying to annoy and hurt him. One day a red squirrel was passing by and heard the evil ones plotting to kill Nanabush's grandmother, who was called Nokomis. The squirrel quickly ran to Nanabush and told him of their plan. Nanabush took his grandmother and hid her in a maple grove, which could only be reached by crossing a narrow log over a waterfall. The Windigoes heard of the hiding place and came looking for Nokomis. When they got to the waterfall, they saw something which was bright red through the mist. They thought it was fire and guessed that Nokomis had been caught in its flames and had perished. They went away believing her to be dead. What they did not know, was that the bright red colour was that of the maple leaves turning with the approach of fall. Nanabush, on hearing of the part that the maples had played in protecting his grandmother, rewarded them by making their sap run sweet and plentifully. This made the maple particularly valuable.

The Origin Of Small Fish

There once was a large sturgeon who was so big that he could swallow a moose, antlers and all, in just one gulp. He was creating much fear among both people and the animals; Nanabush decided to do something about it. He realized that the best way to attack the giant fish was from the inside. He went out into the middle of the lake in a canoe and started to hurl insults at the giant fish. The fish attacked and swallowed both Nanabush and the canoe in which he was standing. Once in the stomach of the fish, Nanabush found that he was not alone. With him were beaver, bear, deer, fox and red squirrel. With red squirrel chattering encouragement, Nanabush attacked the fish's heart. The giant fish soon died and floated to the surface where it was washed to the shore. Birds started to peck at the dead fish and created a hole through which the trapped animals could escape. All of the animals were overjoyed. Nanabush took a knife and cut the dead fish up into lots of little pieces and threw them back into the water. They came alive and started to swim. This was how species of smaller fish came to be. Even to this day red squirrel chatters about this adventure.[5]

These stories about Nanabush paint the picture of a powerful spirit capable of great benevolence. While they believed him to be a teacher of noble values, he also had human failings and was capable of being vengeful.

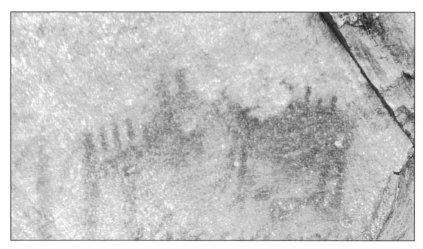

Mishiposhoo (The Great Lynx) ruled over water and protected sacred places.
Courtesy Ministry of Natural Resources.

Other Manitous, or spirts, were also described in legend. At both the north and south end of the pictographs there is a depiction of another one of Kitchi-Manitou's sons, Misshepezhieu, (Mishipashoo) the "Great Lynx." This Manitou's responsibility was to rule over the water and guard sacred places. It was believed that, if someone showed disrespect for a sacred spot, this spirit would stir up the waters and sink the culprit's canoe (While the deterrent seems a bit harsh, its nice to know that Bon Echo, even then, had friends that were willing to provide protection). The Native people offered tobacco with a prayer to Misshepezhieu to appease him before long canoe trips.

Other depictions include Mheehehn (Mikkinuk), "turtle," a fertility symbol. The turtle was thought to be able to communicate between the spiritual and real worlds. According to legend, it acquired this ability from "Sky Woman," a very powerful spirit who once fell from the heavens when the earth was very young and covered with water. The turtle carried her on its back until other creatures could recover mud from the water bottom. Sky Woman spread mud on the turtle's back and blew life into it. It grew until it became the land. Even today, many Native Peoples in North America refer to the continent as Turtle Island. As well, there is another earth creation myth which credits Nanabush with the formation of the land. In both cases the turtle is a prominent feature.

Peenasay was the thunderbird spirit. This Manitou had great power. Because its nest was high on top of the cliffs, it could travel easily between the earth and the spirit world. The thunderbird spirit could assist those on a vision quest by carrying their prayers up from earth. He made thunder by the clapping of his wings and lightening came from his eyes. As this spirit could be either benevolent or punishing, during thunderstorms tobacco and prayer were offered as a form of appeasement.

Also depicted are the Maymaygwayshi, which are lesser spirits, also capable of doing either good or evil. These spirits were thought to live in the crevices of the rocks and cliffs. The story is told of a man

Pictograph often interpreted as Natives in a large canoe. Courtesy Ministry of Natural Resources.

who became concerned when he noticed that fish were being stolen from his nets. One night he saw figures in a canoe paddle out from between the rocks, over to his nets and steal his fish. As they returned towards the cliff, the man blocked their way. As soon as they saw him, they ducked down. The man told them not to be afraid, that he had seen them in his dreams. He asked them why they kept stealing his fish. They replied that fish was their favourite food and that the nets were so good at catching them. The man thought for a moment and then told the spirits that each night, after fishing, he would leave some fish for them. From then on his nets were not bothered.

Water Beings, the May-May-gway-siwuk or mermen, were believed to be spirits who lived in the water. They were very shy and did not like to show their faces. The Native people would offer them tobacco and, in return, the mermen would calm the waters. These beings were also powerful dream guardians. If a person dreamed of these spirits while fasting, he would be given the spiritual strength to resist the power of a sorcerer. The mermen were believed to have knowledge of all matters upon the earth and water. Also it was believed that, a long time ago, the mermen had been warned that one day the white man would come and inhabit the land. When this happened, the mermen would not show themselves anymore because they were afraid that the white man would expose them to public view. The mermen knew, however, that the Ojibwa would still believe in them, even though they would no longer reveal themselves.[6]

The people of the First Nations are not the only ones to have developed legends and myths associated with Mazinaw. A story of lost treasure was taken very seriously in the latter part of the 1800s and the early years of the 1900s. At the time, various versions of the story appeared in the local papers including the *Kingston Whig Standard, Napanee Beaver* and the *Tweed News*. An article in a 1905 edition of the *Tweed News* published the most common version. It was rumoured that the Algonkians had a large amount of silver which they had hidden in a cave. (It wasn't clear whether the cave was simply a hiding place or a mine). They brought some of the silver to a trader called Myers. The Natives claimed that the mine was on top of the Mazinaw Rock. They took Myers there and, after removing moss and rocks which hid the entrance, they brought out silver which they gave to him. Later, they regretted having shown the silver to Myers, and tried to kill him by shoving him over the side of the canoe on the trip back. Myers, somehow, succeeded in swimming to shore and sought help from a settler. He developed pneumonia, however, and died three days later. Before he died, he drew a map showing the cave's approximate location. Other versions of the story say that Myers was a counterfeiter who made bogus coins from the silver he obtained.

This story received broad circulation and there was a lot of searching for the cave, but nothing was ever found. Some versions of the story refer to Walden Myers and others to Captain John Myers. What is known to be true is that Captain John Myers did exist. A United Empire Loyalist, he was a founding father of Belleville, and operated a trading post there, often exchanging goods with Native Peoples.

In the late 1800s, a recluse had a cabin on top of the Rock and lived there for twenty years. He was a prospector who spent much of his time looking for Myers' Cave. According to the writings of Merrill Denison, hardly a summer passed by in the early part of the

1900s that Bon Echo wasn't visited by prospectors. During the summer of 1911, two men from Napanee with the surnames of Scott and Siles, spent almost $10,000 to extensively explore the area after they had been given a clue by a visiting clairvoyant. Late in the summer they found a cave. Scott tumbled in, breaking his leg, but no silver was ever found.[7] More recent geological mapping suggests that it is unlikely that a rich vein of silver was ever discovered in the Mazinaw area. It is possible, however, that Myers came across a silver stash of the Algonkian. The Indians traded in this precious metal. It was considered sacred and their shamans used it to make ceremonial arrowheads.

Denison's papers also mention legends circulated among the early settlers telling of Native maidens who had been forced to leap to their death from the Rock in religious ceremonies of years before, but no evidence has ever been found to support such stories.[8]

From the time of the early pioneers, there have been reported sightings of a large lake creature called the "Mazinaw Monster." Its description varies from a multi-humped serpent to that of a long log-like object that travels swiftly through the water before submerging. Sightings are often at a distance and under less than ideal weather conditions. While probably the product of vivid imaginations and the temptation to impress around the camp fire, the story told by Mont Woods, a county constable for Lennox and Addington, of having sighted a fish the length of a canoe in the Mazinaw, was published in the July 20, 1977 edition of the *Napanee Beaver.* Several years later, he worked for the Ministry of Natural Resources when the Ministry was taking fish counts and using gill nets on the upper lake. One net, when hauled up, had a hole in it one metre (about three feet) wide. Sturgeon live to be 150 years old, can grow to be well over 5 metres or 16 feet in length and weigh 400 to 500 pounds. Mazinaw, with a depth of 137 metres, or about 450 feet, could have produced such a fish.

The spiritual beliefs and legends associated with Bon Echo, both those of the pictographs and of more modern times, are very much a product of the people who created them, reflecting the influences of cultural background, as well as personal hopes, values and prejudices. The Rock is evocative. What is heard or seen, however, is interpreted through the human experience.

LUMBERING THE MIGHTY PINE

1820	Military survey Mazinaw area for lumbering potential
1830 – 1850	Lumbering along the Skootamatta River
1850	Lumber mill established at Flinton
1854	Addington Colonization Road built
1850s	Lumber tramway built from Mazinaw Lake to Pringle Lake and over to the Skootamatta waterway
1860	First dam built at south end of Mazinaw
1860s	Lumbering of giant pine forests well underway
1861	Charles Snider builds lumber chute, gristmill and sawmill at the south end of Mazinaw
1870 to 1890	Greatest period of economic activity supported by lumbering and settlement
1890s	Lumbering declines
1906	Last log drive down the Skootamatta

CHAPTER 3

Lumbering The Mighty Pine

The Mazinaw, because of its relative isolation and the poor soils of its Canadian Shield environment, was one of the last parts of Southern Ontario to be settled. By 1800, logging had started on the Ottawa River with the building of a sawmill at what is now Hull. Beginning in the 1830s, logging proceeded up the Mississippi River from the Ottawa, reaching the Mazinaw in the mid-nineteenth century. By this time, over one million people were living in Canada West, formerly known as Upper Canada. The towns to the south, such as Kingston, Napanee, Belleville and Trenton, were thriving and well-established. Even the lands to the north bordering the Madawaska River, had been lumbered much earlier, due to better access provided by that river.

The area around Flinton, west of Cloyne, may have been logged as early as the 1820s as lumbering progressed up the Moira and Skootamatta watershed. certainly by the 1850s, a lumber mill was established in Flinton and, by 1860, a good road had been constructed from Bridgewater (Actinolite) to supply the lumber trade.

The Mazinaw area, with its great pine forests, was opened by the Addington Colonization Road, which was completed to the lake

and beyond, also during the 1850s. These majestic pines are esti-
mated to have been approximately 400 years old. While the forest
was clear enough for lumber wagons to be driven through the trees,
the forest canopy was so dense that only the occasional shaft of light
penetrated. A springy carpet produced by centuries of fallen pine
needles covered the ground. Interestingly, large trees are reported to
have once grown on top of Bon Echo.[1]

Many of the pine were 38 metres high with a diameter of one
metre or slighly more, and often grew as many as 500 to 800 per
hectare, about 250 to 400 per acre. Cut logs were kept as long as possible, many being 30.5 metres or 100 feet in length. All of the timbers
were squared before being moved down the rivers and nothing was
taken that could not be squared to at least 30 centimetres or 12 inches.
As a result, a great deal of waste was left behind, much of it serving
as kindling for the many local fires that ravaged the area.

By the 1860s, lumbering had become very big business. The size
of investment required and the enormous quantity of logs cut meant
that only well- organized companies, not individuals, could compete
for timber rights. Logging was quite a complex operation requiring
large numbers of men, well-supplied with horses and lumbering

Winter cutting and hauling. Courtesy Tweed Heritage Centre.

equipment. Lumber chutes and dams were built on the rivers and large steam-driven boats were used to haul log booms on the larger lakes, including the Mazinaw. The lumber went to Britain for construction and ship building and, in later years, to both New York City and Chicago which were experiencing construction booms throughout the latter part of the 1800s. [2]

Lumber licences were granted in Barrie township starting in the 1850s. The first firm to log the Mazinaw was the Gilmore Bros. Lumber Company, operating out of Trenton. Others which followed included such well-known names in the lumbering industry as the Gillies, McLaren, Caldwell, Allan and Chandler-Jones companies.

To facilitate its operations, the Gilmore Lumber Company built a tramway on property along the lower Mazinaw, over a parcel of land which would later be owned by Camp Mazinaw. This tramway ran to Pringle Lake and continued on to Skootamatta Lake. Built before 1862, it was later sold to Gillies Bros. and McLaren, as a part of the lumbering rights to the area. Its purpose was to provide a means for hauling logs over to the Skootamatta/Moira waterway. From there, they could be floated down to Lake Ontario and on to Trenton where both the Gilmore and Gillies Bros. lumber companies had mills. The logs were brought up onto the shore at the base of the tramway and then were squared. A chain elevator was used to winch the logs from the shore, up to a landing on top of a rise from which they were put on horse-drawn carriages to be hauled along the tracks to Pringle Lake. Even now, the stone base of this tramway is clearly visible. Approximately 1.8 metres or six feet wide, it slopes at a relatively steep angle at the sides to a base of approximately three metres or ten feet. In many places it is one-and-a-half metres in height. Obviously, this construction was a major engineering effort, a testament to the investment and organizational abilities of the lumber companies.

During the early years of its use, a fire occurred on the shore just where the tramway begins, started when a small blaze, made with green wood to keep the flies away, spread into the shavings.

The original Gillies Bros. Lumber Company was based in

The crosscut saw in action. Courtesy Tweed Heritage Centre.

Scotland, and had lumbering licences on land which stretched from the Gulf of Mexico to the Gatineau region. In 1862, the company acquired the lumbering rights to the area which included the Mazinaw. Each employee who worked in their shanties signed an "Agreement of Employment" spelling out the conditions under which the individual would be hired. In 1877, a general "Working Hand" received $10.00 per month and a first class "Hewer-Clearer" up to $32.00. Many of these agreements were signed with an "X," an indication of the level of literacy in rural Ontario at the time. In September of 1877, Louis Fiset signed such an agreement:

> *I the undersigned do hereby engage to labour and faithfully serve Gillies Bros. or any of their foreman as chainer or general hand and drive logs or timber, raft and go to destination on said logs or timber next season, at the rate of ten dollars per month with the usual shanty board, with the exception of fried pork. I the said Louis Fiset represent and say that I understand and am capable of doing the said description of work above specified and bind myself to the same in a workman-like manner. I further agree to forfeit all wages if I leave*

the employ before the expiration of my agreement, without just cause, or the consent of my employer or foreman, and further, if found not working faithfully, I am liable to be discharged and settled with by due-bill, payable on the arrival of timber or logs at destination.[3]

Initially, Peter McLaren was a manager with Gillies Bros. He later became a partner and, when this partnership ended in 1880, he bought the rights to log the region which included the Mazinaw area.

In 1870, a major dispute erupted between Boyd Caldwell and the McLaren/Gillies partnership with regards as to whether the former could use streams developed by the latter for passing timber. Ultimately, the Provincial Government had to use legislation to establish Caldwell's right to use these waterways, provided appropriate compensation was paid.[4] Simultaneously, there were claims that McLaren's men had burned the dam at Mud Lake, further down the Mississippi chain, thus interfering with the Caldwell operations. These accusations could not be proven in court, however, and tempers continued to run high. There are reports that armed guards were posted at the head of Mazinaw to ensure that rival lumber gangs did not cut the log booms before the boat could take them down the lake.

Piling up the logs along the lake to await the spring run. Courtesy Tweed Heritage Centre.

Log drivers on the Skootamatta. Courtesy Tweed Heritage Centre.

The Mazinaw dam, originally constructed in 1860 at the south end of the lake, was used to maintain water levels for logging. This damming significantly altered the lake's original shoreline, raising the water level by approximately 1.2 metres, about four feet. Originally, the beach at the head of the lake had been a field, a part of the Brown's farm. Before the lake was dammed, the variability of the water level was also far greater: high in the spring and low in the fall. When the loggers wanted to release the logs to travel downstream, they took the retaining timbers out of the dam, thus creating an opening through which the logs could pass. The original dam was located approximately 30 metres north of where the bridge on Head Road is now, and was owned by Issac Allan. In 1900, he sold it to the Chandler-Jones Lumber Company.

Just to the south of the dam was Snider's Depot, the staging area for Charles Snider's operations. A lumber chute, a gristmill and a sawmill were built there in 1861. Eventually, a house, log barns and a warehouse, along with ice and slaughter houses, were added, making it quite an establishment, as illustrated by the capacity of his barns, capable of housing 100 horses. This business was bought, in 1900, by the Canada Lumber Co.[5]

Lumbering was a dangerous occupation. Many deaths occurred, particularly in the spring, as the river drivers worked the logs down-river. When the logs jammed up, they would pile on top of one another below the surface of the water. If a man fell, he would slip under several layers of logs, frequently making rescue impossible. It is known that several lumbermen are buried near the location of Snider's Depot, but the record of the exact location of their graves has been lost.

The pond and river between Mazinaw and Little Marble Lake contain three archaeological sites which hold promise for the recovery of artifacts from the lumbering days. So far, machine-wrought iron nails, ceramics and a hand-forged U-bolt have been recovered. The Mississippi River Conservation Authority maintains an active interest in preservation of these sites.

Other than the foreman, the most important person in the lumbering camp was the cook. Typically, the camboose (lumber camp) was built on sand around a cook fire, with heavy pieces of timber surrounding the cooking pit. The smoke from the large fire kept burning in the centre escaped through a hole in the roof. Day after day, the same type of food was served: beans, salt pork and a form of bannock bread, all cooked in big pots. Food was eaten from tin plates held on the knees. Sometimes the men even had to bring their own tea and sugar. To prevent scurvy, spruce bud tea was often drunk, a practice adopted from the Aboriginals. Each day, the noon meal was eaten in the bush and only in the evening would the men return to camp.

The camps along the Mississippi were rough places. Men worked long hours, six or seven days a week, and lights were out by nine. Often beds were a blanket spread over spruce branches, with a coat for a pillow. Most of the men had no baths all winter. Although life was hard, they made their own fun with much step-dancing, singing, contests of strength and story telling. Today, many of their tall tales and songs form part of Canada's lumbering heritage. Alcohol was frowned upon by the camp bosses, but when the men were paid at the end of the season, they would often hit the nearby towns for

"Decking" the logs onto platforms to await spring, Abinger township, circa 1890. Courtesy Lennox and Addington County Museum.

drinking binges, creating annual events which sometimes turned violent. There are certainly many stories of brawls between men of the rival lumber companies of the times, along both the Mississippi and the Madawaska rivers.

Records from the Gillies Bros. Lumber Company for the year 1890 provide an indication of the type of supplies ordered for their shanties. In addition to food, cooking utensils and blankets, other items were included: rope; chains; lamp chimneys and wick; wooden pails; tin plates; resin; hand-wrought nails; coal oil; broad axes; scoring saws; iron bars; lead marking pencils; stove black; sealing wax; toilet soap; pitch; cross-cut saws; harness leather and straw hats.[6]

These logging shanties were staffed both by homesteaders, who needed winter employment, and by the more permanent employees of the lumber companies, the latter migrating to wherever trees were being logged. Each man had his own specific job to do. The men who cut down the trees were referred to as sawyers. They used crosscut saws and axes weighing as much as two kilograms or five pounds each. Teamsters with horses or oxen were employed to haul the logs, with each man being responsible for his own team. Chains were used and the team would pull the logs to where they were needed. In winter, loads of logs were hauled on sleighs to skidways on the shore of a lake or stream, to be driven downstream at spring breakup. Blacksmiths also were needed to produce and repair tools and equipment. Once the logs had been piled on the shore or ice, the job of the lumberjack was finished. It was now up to the log driver to take the timber down stream.

Wilfred Lessard, a local historian, born in 1895 in Flinton, described the difference between these two jobs in his book, *The Village On The Skoot*:

> *The accommodation for the early log driver was cotton tents in which the driver slept on boughs, insulating him from the cold ground. The food was of the same quality and preparation as that of the shanty, except that the cooking was outdoors. Not all lumberjacks were log drivers. They didn't all work in the two operations of the lumbering industry and this was due to the choice of the foreman and the individual. In the shanty it was brawn and muscle and on the drive it was skill of balance and speed. It commanded the better pay of $2 to $4 per month. That brought resentment and envy resulting in the slurry names of riverhogs for the drivers and woodbutchers for the lumberjacks.[7]*

The logs were moved downstream by a system called "impounding." Water was dammed to raise the water level. Once the logs reached the dam, the water was released, allowing them to be floated down to the next dam or impounding site.

Originally, log booms on the Mazinaw were hauled down the lake attached to a wooden crib cage, a type of raft measuring 12 metres by 12 metres equipped with an anchor on a long rope. The anchor was dropped some distance ahead of a boom and the crib cage towed back to the boom while the rope was let out. The crib cage was then attached to the boom, and two horses in harness would reel in the rope by walking in a circle around a capstan, a revolving barrel with spokes to which the horses were tethered. This process was repeated numerous times. The lumber booms were assembled at the head of the lake and taken down to the Narrows, where the boom was undone and the logs floated through in small groups. The boom was then reassembled and taken down to the foot of the lake.[8]

During the late 19th century, the Canada Lumber Company (Peter McLaren) kept a large steamboat on the lake. It replaced the need for the wooden crib. During the summer, when the lumbering had been completed, the boat was used to take folks from Cloyne and the surrounding area out for evening cruises, often with a fiddle player supplying entertainment. According to the book, *The Oxen And The Axe*, the steamer was 23 metres long and could hold 100 people. In 1906, when the dam at the bottom of the lake went out, the steamer was washed downstream and broke up just before the rapids at the entrance to Little Marble Lake, where its remains still rest in approximately nine metres or about 30 feet of water.

Elsewhere in the province, the lumber companies often used what was referred to as an alligator tug. This craft, invented in 1889 by John West of Simcoe, Ontario, had large paddlewheels on each side. There also were skids on its bottom to protect the boat while going over shallows. The alligator boat, with its 1.6 kilometres or one mile of steel cable and 500 pound anchor, moved the log booms by dropping the anchor some distance down lake and then returning to the boom. Once attached, the boat would winch itself back to where the anchor had been dropped. This process would then be repeated. The boat could also winch itself over land, using the power generated from its steam boiler. To accomplish this, the cable was tied to a tree and logs were placed on the ground at intervals of about two to two-and-half metres. The flat hull of the boat was greased and the boat then winched forward. Today, in Algonquin Park, the rotting remains of these boats can still be found, and a restored alligator tug is on display in the town of Simcoe as a reminder of a bygone era.

From 1870 to 1890, the Mazinaw area experienced its greatest economic boom, a prosperity based on lumbering and farming. By the late 1890s, however, the major lumbering operations had started to move further north, leaving smaller firms, such as T.A. Wilson and the Wells Bros., to log what remained. While the Sawyer-Stoll Lumber Company would later be active in the area, large scale lumbering was on the decline, causing the market for local agriculture to simultaneously dwindle.

Today, lumbering is of little significance in the local economy although some controlled logging still does exist. Currently, there are small-scale lumbering operations in the area just north of Bon Echo Provincial Park. As the current forest continues to mature, however, the harvesting of certain species will become increasingly viable. Indeed there is, at present, increasing pressure to grant lumbering rights. The responsibility for ensuring an appropriate balance between lumbering and the protection of the forest as habitat for wildlife and for recreational use falls to the provincial Ministry of Natural Resources.

SETTLEMENT ALONG THE
COLONIZATION ROAD (1854-1899)

1854 – 1856	Addington Colonization Road built
1859	179 free land grants to settlers had been issued along the road
1862 – 1864	Drought particularly hard on early settlers
1864	Wickware House built as local hotel
1865	Tapping family receives land grant just north of the Narrows
1868	First school built just north of Cloyne
1870	First of three churches built in Cloyne
1870 to 1890	Greatest period of economic activity supported by lumbering and settlement
1882	CPR railway built through Kaladar
1895	First known painting of Bon Echo by R.J. Drummond
1899	Bon Echo Inn built

CHAPTER 4

Settlement Along
the Colonization Road

After the War of 1812, the British, realizing they were vulnerable to American naval attack on Lake Ontario, wanted to establish navigation routes well back from this body of water. There was support, in the early 1820s, for making the Mississippi navigable and connecting it to other river systems through the Mazinaw. To the south, it was to be linked to Skootamatta Lake and then down the Skootamatta River to join with the Moira River, thus providing access to Lake Ontario at Belleville. To the northwest, it was to connect with Effingham Lake, continue on to Weslemkoon Lake, then to the York, a tributary of the Madawaska River, eventually providing access to Lake Simcoe. The concept was researched by Samuel Clowes, a provincial civil engineer, who also was involved with the building of the Rideau Canal. The proposal proved to be too costly, however, and settlement was postponed another 30 years.[1]

During the 1830s, the military did a reconnaissance of the area to estimate its forestry potential for the lumbering trade. Although a few trappers' cabins were encountered, they found the region relatively untouched.

Settlement finally came to the Mazinaw in the 1850s, in conjunction with the lumbering boom, although there had been some earlier settlement closer to Flinton ten years before. The lumber companies encouraged settlement as a source of local farm produce, of winter labourers and of tradespeople, all close at hand. A combination of petitions from the lumber firms and mounting concerns about the growing number of Canadians leaving to settle in the United States led the government to build colonization roads running back from the "front," the shoreline of Lake Ontario.

The Addington Road, not built until 1854, was one of the last of the colonization roads to be developed. Today, its construction is commemorated with an historical plaque in Kaladar, a testament to its local significance. The surveyor and contractor for the work was Aylsworth (A.B.) Perry. Although not a local resident, he assigned the area around Mazinaw Lake facing Bon Echo as the site for his personal homestead. Meanwhile, it was his brother, Ebenezer, appointed as land agent who was responsible for encouraging settlement.

Initially, the road was surveyed from Clareview, just north of Napanee, to the Madawaska River. In later years it was extended further north. During the first year approximately 76 kilometres or 45 miles were built at a cost of 53 pounds sterling per mile. Two years later, in April of 1856, the building of a bridge over the Madawaska marked the completion of the first stage.

In reality, this new road was little better than a rough broad trail. Reduced to a corduroy road in the swampy parts, much of the rest was rocky and rutted and only accessible to ox carts or lumber wagons or people on foot. Travellers had to contend with icy grades in the winter, mud holes in the spring and dust in the summer. With many of the stumps still remaining in the pathway, carts or any wheeled conveyance had to be driven around them. Often, it was easier to travel the road in winter, using sleighs over the snow and ice. Even then, the trip from Kaladar to Denbigh could take the better part of two days to complete. Despite these hardships, travel on the road increased and, by 1857, there were often 20 teams of horses counted, coming and going each day. That same year there were 225 horse and oxen teams engaged in hauling and skidding logs along the road from Kaladar to the head of the Mazinaw.[2]

Settlers, who met certain conditions, were granted 40 hectare (100 acre) lots, these sections of land having been surveyed with little regard for their agricultural potential. Successful candidates had to be male, at least 18 years of age, take possession of their land within one month and agree to construct a cabin at least six by five-and -a half metres within the year. They also had to reside on the property and have five hectares (12 acres) under cultivation within four years, as well as help with the maintenance of the colonization road.

Five men (usually the help came from the neighbours) could put up the required home in four days. The walls of these cabins were made of logs with the chinks being stuffed with moss or plastered with clay. Overhead, the roofs were often shingled with pieces of wood shaped in the form of overlapping troughs. The lower portion of the chimney was built of stone and the upper section constructed from pieces of split cedar, something like lath, and plastered on the inside with clay. In the early years, with no local sawmill nearby, the floor boards for cabins had to be hauled in by wagon.

Even with neighbourly assistance, meeting these conditions was not an easy task. As the following letter to Ebenezer Perry attests, settlers often met with unforseen circumstances:

December 20, 1857
E. Perry
Dear Sir,

I find it impossible for me to meet the obligation to work upon the land as soon as I thought to have done when I left on account of bad sleighing which we have here. As soon as the sleighing will admit, I shall return to the land that I have taken up and do up the duty according to the Government requirement. The calculation with us here is that my father and brother will come with me in order to make

a home for ourselves there. I therefore hope that you will be so kind
as to hold the land for us, the three lots namely 28 and 29 in Anglesy
and 30 in Barrie. Your compliance with the above would confer a great
favour on your most obedient and humble servant.

Charley B. Cornell[3]

While the settlers were from varied backgrounds, all were drawn
by the enticement of free land and an opportunity to build a better
life for themselves and their children. Most had scanty farming
background and were ill-prepared for the hardships which awaited
them. Five years after the opening of the colonization road, 179 free
grants had been given to settlers along the Addington: 89 of them
were from Canada West; 19 from Canada East; 26 from Ireland; 4
from Prussia; 1 from Cape Breton; 11 from the U.S.; 24 from
England; 4 from Scotland and 1 from Denmark.[4]

A.B. Perry's assessment of the agricultural potential of the region
was far too optimistic. He described two types of soil: yellow sand,
good for growing pines; and dark loams, which he claimed were very

Hans Karterfeldt was famous around Kaladar for his mixed team. Courtesy
Lennox and Addington County Museum

productive, capable of supporting the cultivation of a variety of crops. He did indicate, however, that the area also contained many swamps and poorly drained bogs, as well as rocky land, all unsuitable for agriculture. Perry was not alone in being overly optimistic. Many early settlers had the mistaken impression that, because the land could grow huge trees, it would be good for growing crops. What they failed to recognize was that such massive trees could survive in the thin glacial soil only because of their matted root systems. Once the trees were cut down and the roots died, the soil became vulnerable to erosion. As well, the region's ability to sustain agriculture was also devastated by the repeated occurence of many fires, continously depleting the thin top soil.

In the early years, however, the settlers were able to provide for themselves reasonably well, growing a variety of grains, corn, buckwheat, turnips and hay, and, of course, the essential vegetable garden. A monthly report on the Addington Road, in 1858, indicates that, in addition to the planting of crops, a number of apple orchards had been planted. The report also notes that fifty-eight deer had been killed in that month, likely venison to supplement their diet.[5]

The weather in both 1862 and 1864 was extraordinarily bad, the combination of a late frost and an early drought in 1862 particularily devastating for the farmers. To give some much needed employment, the government began work on a northward extension of the Addington Road. In 1864, another drought, with no rainfall for the six weeks from the beginning of June to mid-July, added to the hardship. Although construction work on the Addington still provided some paid work, the settlers began to realize more fully the difficult sacrifices which survival in this country could demand. The spring of the year was hardest. Many had nothing but turnips to eat. Some did not even have seed for the next planting. For many, winter supplies had been used up and gardens were not yet in production. The year 1862 saw twelve settlers abandon their homesteads and only five lots were taken up. During the following year, a total of 33 more settlers left and, by 1864, no new lots were being claimed.[6]

Life required a stamina which is now hard to imagine. With very few horses available in the early years, the poorer settlers had to walk to Newburg, north of Napanee, or to Bridgewater (Actinolite) for supplies. Corn and grain had to be taken to Comer's Mills, east of Northbrook, or to Bridgewater to be ground. Death was a constant companion. As in other early settlements throughout Ontario, many women died during childbirth and the infant mortality rate was very high. A cemetery on the Marble Lake Road, close to Myers Cave, contains a number of the early graves, a vivid reminder of these harsh conditions.

Frequently, farmers settled on soil which had been logged. While more clearing was still needed, the larger pines were gone. The family's first cash crop was usually potash, a product easy to make by using debris left from the lumbering and the remaining trees yet to be cleared. The resulting barrels of potash would be sold for other supplies, and thus were often what supported the settler through that first winter.

To supplement the fodder supply for cattle, early farmers made use of what was referred to as wild beaver or marsh hay. This wild hay was not of a high quality, but was harvested by those with low-lying land with little other potential. Spring burning was introduced as a means to produce both a higher quality and quantity of marsh hay, and also to improve the yields of grass for grazing on upland areas. While this practice did improve production in the short term, in reality, it contributed to the overall depletion of the rocky, shallow soils.

Families had to make do with products, often either made at home or acquired locally. Clothes, soap, candles, furniture, many household utensils and pieces of farm equipment were all made by hand. Pot cheese was made by souring milk, adding sugar, salt and pepper, boiling the mixture and then squeezing it by hand to remove the water. The first step in producing soft soap for washing clothes was to save the fat (tallow) from beef. Next, water would be poured over wood ashes to leach out the lye, then strained and mixed with the tallow. Finally, the mixture would be boiled down. Each fireplace was equipped with a hinged iron bar, used to suspend a cooking pot. For baking, this cooking pot would be set in red-hot coals.

Stoneboats, which resembling flat wooden rafts, were used in clearing stone from the fields. This useful but unpretentious piece of equipment was drawn by a single horse, and the farm children were expected to walk beside it, helping with this onerous task. Today, piles and piles of stone can be seen along old fence rows, the product of hours and hours of back-breaking labour. Another essential farm activity was the sharpening of axes, scythes, knives and other tools. While it would be necessary to purchase the grinding stone, the frame and turning handles usually were made right on the farm.

Storage of food for both the long harsh winters and hot summer days was a challenge. Fruits and vegetables were dried or canned and meat was smoked or pickled. A structure known as a root house was often built into the side of a hill and was used to store root vegetables such as turnips, carrots, potatoes and beets, as well as cabbage and apples. In early spring, a sorting would take place. Spoiled food was thrown out and sprouted potatoes were put aside for spring planting. Those with farms on flat land, with no hill into which to excavate, constructed root cellars which, once dug into the ground, served the same purpose.

Many of the early farmers also built ice houses. A large-toothed saw approximately one-and-a-half metres in length, with a handle at one end, was used to cut the winter ice into large blocks. These blocks were hauled to the ice house, liberally covered in sawdust and left there for future use. If properly stored, this ice would last the whole summer.

In 1865, Thomas Tapping received a land grant of 40 hectares (96 acres) just north of the Narrows. The fields of his farm are still in evidence today. As you drive into Bon Echo Park, turn to your left into the large parking lot and follow the foot path which leads north. This is the same path that leads to the High Pines Trail. Tapping became the first postmaster in the area. For some obscure reason, the Tapping farm post office was called "Hardinge" by the federal government of the day. He also became Barrie township's first reeve, thus becoming a man of some influence in the community. Like most of the other settlers, the Tappings provided the lumber companies with farm produce.[7]

Although life during these times was difficult at best, there are early reports which describe a growing sense of community in the village of Cloyne. A Methodist church was constructed in 1870 and an Anglican church shortly afterwards. Even after the churches were built, the settlements continued to be served by itinerant ministers who came through on horseback. Because their visits were few and far between, they often appointed lay people to act in their place. Community cohesiveness was strengthened by the many dinners and social gatherings held at the town hall and church centres. Sleigh rides, barn raisings and corn roasts were all part of that which made life memorable. One such event was the potato harvesting party held annually at the Tapping farm. The first school, constructed in 1868 at the corner of the old Addington Road and Loon Lake (Skootamatta) Road, also added to the feeling of permanence and stability.

As settlement took root, travelling peddlars made their appearance. Some had horse-drawn carts while others just carried packs on their backs. The pack peddlars loaded up with light things like needles, thread, ribbons, buttons, reading glasses and inexpensive jewellery.

From 1855 to 1870, a span of fifteen years, full-scale lumbering developed in the Mazinaw region and provided both a ready market for farm produce and a source of winter employment. Correspondingly, the area population stabilized, and would reach its peak in the 1880s. From the 1870s to the turn of the century, lumbering combined with agriculture to provide a period of sustained economic activity; a time when a settler could provide a reasonable livelihood for his family, had he been fortunate enough to have received a grant of land capable of sustaining crops.

While this relationship between settlers and lumber companies was mutually beneficial, it was not without tension. In his annual report for 1863, Ebenezer Perry tells of conflicts. Sometimes, settlers would infringe on the lumber company's timber rights in order to obtain sufficient wood for the making of potash. On the other hand, lumber companies would often ignore the property rights of settlers while pursuing their logging operations.

As local services were established, life became easier. Blacksmiths not only provided shoes for horses but repaired farm equipment, cooking pots and other household implements. One such blacksmith was George Wheeler, who had his shop in Cloyne where Nowell's garage now stands. By 1880, this village also had a flour and feed dealer, a tin shop, a livery stable, two carpenter's shops, a wagon maker, a general store, a hotel and an agriculture implement maker. A horse-drawn stage driven by John William McCausland, travelled from Kaladar to Cloyne during the late 1800s, thus strengthening Cloyne's connection to the outside world. McCausland's homestead was located just to the north of Marble Lake, south of the Mazinaw. A long-time resident and well-known personality, his name remains in the area as McCausland Lake.

Bill Head, who married the daughter of J. W. McCausland, left his name to Head Road at the south end of the Mazinaw. They later inherited her family homestead and, eventually, it became known as the Head Place. Bill served in municipal politics and ultimately took over the job of driving the coach from Kaladar to Cloyne.

The Wickware House, built in 1864, was the local hotel in Cloyne. It survived for almost 100 years before being consumed by fire in 1963. As well, another establishment called the Spencer Hotel operated at the head of the lake from 1873 to 1903. It housed lumbermen and could accommodate up to 50 people in its dining room. According to the book, *The Oxen and the Axe*, some of the men who died in logging accidents were brought to the hotel, and were buried in a field slightly less than a kilometre south of the head of the lake. The bones of several of these bodies were later exposed when the water level of the lake was raised and the shore eroded. The location of this burial site, however, does not appear in any government records of cemeteries from that period, nor does anyone seem to know what happened to these human remains.

In the summer and early fall of 1876, Samuel Lane was the overseer of a construction crew, assigned by the government to do
repairs on the Addington Road. Their labour that summer was
tough: making culverts; hauling earth and stone; building up the
road in low and washed-out sections; filling in the numerous wagon
ruts; cutting fallen trees and moving them out of the way, all done
with only the most basic of tools. Logs were put in place to re- corduroy wet boggy areas. They cleared wider margins for the road,
cut roots, filled pitch holes, grubbed-out stumps, graded and made
water courses to drain water away. Passages from Lane's work diary
provide insights into the condition of the road some twenty years
after it had first been constructed:

July 8
The Addington Road in vicinity is as bad a specimen of road as could
be found in the Province. This day is very hot. Thermometer 85 degrees
in the shade, one man sick had to lay up

July 18
Thermometer 98 degrees in the shade, but plenty of good pork and
bread appears to keep my men in heart although [they] *suffer from*
the heat and mosquitoes

July 20
Going ahead, new piece of road will be completed this evening.
Thunder and rain at 10 o'clock cooled the air. Very hot again in the
afternoon. We have reached free grant lot 26 and expect to reach 28
this evening. This lot 28 and also 29 is in possession of a half crazy
doctor called Doey, dissatisfied with every man and every man dis-
satisfied with him. He lives a hermit. Thinks government, council and
every department in Canada all humbug

July 22
Closely examined this hill [Eagle Hill – located between the
head of the Mazinaw and the village of Vennachar] *this day*

and find it shall require much labour to improve it. In its present state it is the terror of teams and teamsters. No wagon can be made to stand it a few times. If I can succeed in turning and keeping the water from running down it, I shall do well as every work put on it for the past has washed clearly away leaving it like the bed of an old river. The assent in some places is 10 feet [rise] *for every 16 feet and boulders step after step*

September 11
Same work as Saturday. Team sent to Cloyne for pork and flour. One horse team drawing firewood for cook.

September 13
Employed this day as before, made a few rods of progress. I wish the Commission could see this road for even ten minutes. I am not surprised that setters turn away from our section of the country in terror but thanks to this grant, as far as it goes, it will effect a considerable improvement.

September 15
Terrible piece of road before us this day. The road excavated by floods three feet from the original level of it and a wall of immense boulders piled up at each side by former workers. But we are overcoming those difficulties by degrees. The men and foreman work well and I try to be on the road in the midst all the time.

September 22
The road has become narrow and dangerous. . . . We shall be obliged to break off three or four feet of rock at the upper side, which we shall have to effect with iron bars and sledges [work done by hand with no dynamite or air pressure tools].

September 26
Ox team employed drawing guard logs for this place being a precipice over 30 feet below it.

September 28
I have used up all the tools, picks, bars, spades, axes, and shovels. We shall require a new set next year [if the grant is renewed].

October 2
Concluding diary – no drunkenness, no quarrels, breakfast at 5 o'clock, at work at 6 o'clock, dinner at 11 o'clock, at work at 12 and to 6 o'clock, then supper.[8]

Like many other unorganized and remote regions of the country, the administration of the law during this period left much to be desired. Magistrate positions were patronage appointments made by the government with only cursory attention given to qualifications. Constables, appointed by the county, usually were untrained. Often, they would hesitate to go against local opinion or to put themselves in harm's way. They did, however, have power of arrest and the responsibility of custody of any prisoner until trial. Poor roads and long distances frequently meant that a prisoner would be kept in the constable's home, an arrangement not conducive to rigorous enforcement of the law. While most of the settlers were law-abiding and community-minded, some took advantage of this inadequate law enforcement. Seemingly, the hardships of the time brought out both the best and worst in people.

Wilfred Lessard, in his book on Flinton, *The Village on the Skoot*, makes reference to a variety of early crimes including murder, rape, armed robbery, feuding, horse stealing, domestic disputes and arson. According to Lessard, sometime before 1850, Triffle Goyette, an early white settler, abducted a young Native girl and took her back to his cabin near Flint's Falls (later to be called Flinton). The girl's family and their friends set after Triffle, rope in hand, with the intention of lynching him. Fortunately for Goyette, they were kept at a distance by his domesticated wolf. Probably wisely, Triffle, frightened by the threats of the girl's family, returned her to them shortly thereafter. She later became the mother of his son Joe.

Another of his accounts is of a Jewish jewellery peddlar named Steinburg who, in 1859, was travelling through the area selling his wares to the settlers and to men in the lumbering camps. He boarded for a time at the home of a couple known as the Elwoods. Shortly thereafter, Steinburg went missing and the Elwoods could be seen riding about the country, driving the peddlar's horse and buckboard. Suspicion mounted, but there was not enough evidence to prosecute. The Elwoods soon left the area, but were later arrested near Belleville where they had murdered a man, decapitating him with a hay scythe. This time, they were brought to quick justice and sentenced to the gallows. Just before the execution, the wife confessed to the earlier murder of Steinburg in Flinton.

Lessard also makes mention of a murder which occurred just north of Cloyne during the deer season of 1899. Pete Hawley was found shot to death while manning a deer runway at the outlet of Skootamatta Lake. His rifle had an unspent cartridge in the breech, so it was concluded that he had been murdered. Indeed, Hawley had been in dispute with some other local hunters regarding this favourite hunting spot. While the case was investigated, no charges were ever laid; the identity of the murderer remaining a source of mystery and local speculation.

In 1884, the Canadian Pacific Railway was extended through Kaladar. Until a station and rail sidings were built, there was little to mark the hamlet's existence other than a hotel and a post office. Up to that time the settlement had been known as Scouten, named after Silas Scouten, an early settler in the area. With the arrival of the rail line, the community was renamed Kaladar Station. Five years later, the village had a general store, flour mill and sawmill. The name change to Kaladar Station created a problem, however, because some time earlier, Northbrook had been assigned the name of Kaladar. It was very confusing to have one village named Kaladar Station and the other named Kaladar. Something had to be done; thus the name of Northbrook was introduced. Name changes were nothing new for Northbrook which previously had been referred to by a number of names including: Dunham's Place, Dunham's Corners, Beaverbrook and Springbrook.[9]

The coming of the railway created a number of local jobs for both the station's requirements and the maintenance of the line. As well, agricultural goods could now be taken to the railway for shipment and manufactured goods could be ordered by catalogue and picked up locally. One of the prime cargoes on this line was western grain, shipped by freighter from Thunder Bay on Lake Superior, through the locks at Sault Ste. Marie and on to Port McNichol on Georgian Bay. There, it was loaded on trains and shipped by rail to Montreal, the nearest ocean port before the building of the St. Lawrence Seaway. According to Wilfred Lessard, it was not unusual during the navigational season on the Great Lakes, to see as many as 20 wheat trains pass through Kaladar, travelling seven minutes apart as established by a signal dispatcher's order: "This was when groups of boys travelled by foot from the vicinity of Flinton through the woods and over hills to what was known as number five grade, about five kilometres (three miles) west of the station and there smeared the rails with wagon grease that ground the train to a dead stop. The engineers of the trains leaped from the cabs raining unwritable invectives from their frothing mouths."[10]

The CPR built a second rail line along the shore of Lake Ontario in 1915. Once this southern line was in place, the Kaladar train traffic fell off and the maintenance crews stationed there were relocated.

While the focus of the day was on lumbering and agriculture, signs of future tourism were starting to emerge. The Bon Echo Inn would not be built until 1899, but, as the area was opened up, word of the Mazinaw slowly spread, attracting the infrequent but intrepid adventurer. At the Park's Visitor Centre, hangs the first known picture of the Rock. It was painted in 1895 by R.J. Drummond, who was managing the Bank of Montreal in Perth at the time. He and a companion travelled up the Mississippi in two birchbark canoes. The Rock in the painting looks just the same as it does today, except that the water level appears to be lower.

Awaiting the train at Kaladar Station. Courtesy Lennox and Addington County Museum.

In describing the Rock, Drummond wrote:

When 12 o'clock comes the sun glints from the long line of its top lengthening down its face and as the sun westerly moves, the lights grow longer, down to the base, and broad shadows dissect it into many rocks, each lichened and mossed with velvet, brown and gold and on which the little cedars cling sweetly, with silent submission, stunted growth but sure foundation and the sun makes features and faces out of the fractures of frost and time and the Indian has painted the base. We sat till the afternoon brought colour into the sunlight and the lake mirrored its lighted fractures and its shadowed ridges and the water was as deep as the rock turned downward, and the birds crossed the sky below its mirrored outline and the lake northward was floating its distant shores so like shadowy gossamer a little breeze might wreck them. In the stillness a good ear could hear the loons calling from its head, five miles away.[11]

Billa Flint (1805-1894)

The son of Billa and Phoebe (Wells) Flint, he was born in Elizabethtown (Brockville) in 1805. Billa Flint moved to Belleville in 1829 and rapidly became a key industrial player in eastern Ontario. Courtesy Tweed Heritage Centre.

Flinton is a much older settlement than the villages found along Highway 41. The first few settlers may have established homesteads as early as 1844. Certainly the area was known to the Mohawk people, fur traders and lumber estimators who used the old Indian trail along the Moira and Skootamatta rivers to gain access. The village, established beside a lumber mill on the Skootamatta River, was named after Billa Flint, an early lumber baron from Belleville, who was later to become a member of the Canadian Senate.

Billa Flint was a colourful, deal-making business tycoon who originally had made a considerable amount of money in lumbering interests throughout the county of Hastings. He was a hard-driving man with a strong personality and a puritan streak. A reformist politically, he had a zeal for temperance and strictly observed the Sabbath. He was particularly active in Bridgewater (Actinolite) where he had built a number of businesses, including a flour mill and factory facilities for the manufacture of axes, scythes, hammers, ox yokes and shoes for both oxen and horses. He also owned a combination textile and garment factory in the same location.

In 1852, Billa Flint started lumbering operations in the Flinton area. Three years later, he constructed a combined flour and sawmill and a company store along the shores of the Skootamatta River, thus establishing Flint Mills, later to be known as Flinton. He attempted to consolidate his interests in both Bridgewater and Flint Mills by improving the road, the old Indian trail, that connected them. Later, he would build a new road to shorten the distance. Flint commissioned a survey in 1859 to establish a village site. Evidence of his influence and generosity is seen in his donations of land, including two lots for the Methodist church and manse, two lots for the school, one for the town hall and another for a cemetery. But along with his generosity came power as demonstrated in his use of leverage to prohibit the sale of alcohol in the village.

The fortunes of Billa Flint soured following a series of disasters. His attempt to have a railway line built through Bridgewater failed; his mills at that location were destroyed by fire in 1879, and his other business setbacks, including a failed mining venture with the grandfather of Merrill Denison, were just too much. Eventually, he found himself unable to meet either his many payrolls or his business debts. He withdrew from commerce entirely to spend his few remaining years travelling back and forth from his home in Belleville to the Senate in Ottawa. Billa Flint died in 1882. Curiously, the once flamboyant personality seems to have all but disappeared from public record, even his burial site was difficult to locate.

A number of French Canadians worked in Flint's lumbering operations and in those of the Gilmore Lumber Company. Many built homes in a hamlet called the French Settlement located between Highway 41 and Flinton. A number of these settlers were buried in the cemetery beside the Catholic Church. To this day, a number of French family names are common in the area.[12]

About 16 kilometres north of the Mazinaw lies Denbigh, a very picturesque village, situated close to the shore of a small lake of the same name. Paul Stein, in 1910, completed an unpublished manuscript entitled, "History of the Back End of Addington County." In it he describes the early history of this community and the beginnings of its German heritage:

> *In order to attract German immigrants to Upper Canada, the government had issued some German literature which was distributed by Immigration Agents in Germany, in which the newly opened districts adjoining the Frontenac, Addington and Hastings Colonization roads were very favourably described and recommended for settlers with limited means. One of the pamphlets fell into the hands of two neighbours in the Prussian province of Silesia, who were at once very favourably impressed with the statement that they could get each one hundred acres of good land which, when cleared, would grow every kind of farm produce that was raised in their own native province for nothing; and though they were not practical farmers, for one of them, Charles Heuman, was . . . foreman in a distillery and the other August John, was a miller who had only a small gristmill rented, they decided to try their luck in Canada. Crossing the Atlantic in the 1850s in the steerage of an immigrant sailing vessel in which they had to furnish their own provisions, bedding for the trip lasting from seven to ten weeks and in one case with smallpox and no physician on board ship, thirteen weeks, was no trifle; but they landed safely in Quebec, reached Napanee, where they with the assistance of a countryman, who acted as their interpreter, purchased the necessary supplies and engaged a couple of teams which brought them to their destination in Denbigh Township in the summer of 1858. They took possession of and located on adjoining lots on the Addington road, built with the help of neighbours a log shanty large enough to hold both families and all their possessions, and went to work with a will to clear yet a little land for a late crop of turnips and some other roots. They were the first pioneers of what was years afterwards known as the German, or Dutch, settlement. But they were destined to meet with a very serious misfortune. Intending to acquire cows, they all, men, women and children, left the shanty one morning in the early fall to cut some hay in a Beaver meadow quite a distance from it [the shanty]. While*

thus engaged they happened to look towards their habitation and noticed a heavy column of smoke rising in that direction. Hurrying home they found their dwelling with all contents a mass of flames, out of which they were not able to save a particle, and had nothing left but their poorest clothes they dressed themselves with in the morning. A pitiful situation for anyone but how much more as for those two families with a couple of little children each in a strange country, in the forest away from almost all civilization! After consulting what to do next, Mr. Neuman decided to remain and to try his luck in trapping and hunting, while Mr. John preferred to move with his family to Bridgewater [Actinolite], where both he and his wife found employment. In the following spring they returned to their homestead and built a small log cabin for themselves In 1860 and 1861, several other German families joined them, and they began to feel more at home. They laboured, however, under many serious disadvantages.

Their nearest post office was at Perry's Mills and afterwards at Hardinge in the Township of Barrie, a distance of over twenty miles. In 1863 Denbigh post office was established with David Hughes as postmaster and Gottard Radel as the first mail carrier, who had to carry the mail on foot there being as yet no horses in the settlement. Another great disadvantage was the want of a grist mill, the nearest one being in Bridgewater.[13]

It was not uncommon for a farmer to charge his neighbours one bag of grain for every two bags to be transported to the mill. While this may seem harsh, it must be remembered that the price was a reflection of just how difficult it was to make the approximately 56 kilometre trip, a distance of about 35 miles over rough and treacherous terrain.

By 1902 the town [Denbigh] contained a roller mill, one steam sawmill, three general stores, two public or boarding houses, two churches, one public school, two blacksmiths shops, one woodworking shop, two agencies for agricultural implements, one physician, one

The Crabtree homestead near Denbigh circa 1890. Courtesy Lennox and
Addington County Museum.

*crown land office, a post office, one Orange Hall, and two public halls
belonging to private owners and a cheese factory.*[14]

One of the more difficult stretches of the Addington Road,
described earlier by Samuel Lane, was Eagle Hill located near the settlement of Vennacher, between the Mazinaw and Denbigh. In rainy
weather, it was almost impassable. Over the years, many improvements have been made to this particular stretch of roadway, but even
with the most modern of construction techniques and equipment,
it has never been completely tamed. In the spring flooding of 1998,
it was at Eagle Hill that Highway 41 was completely washed away,
pavement, gravel bed and all.

In some respects, the experiences of settlers in the Mazinaw
region were similar to those of others who had homesteaded in the
more accessible parts of Southern Ontario years before. By 1900,
Ontario's larger cities were bustling with commerce, as the province
started to industrialize. Good roads and the building of the railways
greatly aided the transporting of goods and people, and economic

conditions improved. However, because of its rugged Canadian Shield environment, with a lack of land suitable for agriculture and its isolated location, the people of the Mazinaw region were not experiencing this same growth. Indeed, for them even harder times lay ahead.

CONTINUING SETTLEMENT (1901 – 1939)

Early 1900s	Exodus of settlers as lumbering companies depart
1900 – 1936	Mining exploration and small scale mining operations
1901	Bon Echo Inn completed and opened for business
1920	Trip from Kaladar to Cloyne takes one and three quarter hours
1933	Highway 7 opens as a provincial highway
1935	Highway 41 (the former Addington Colonization Road) completed
1939	Hydro introduced

CHAPTER 5

Continuing Settlement

By the end of the 1800s, the landscape in the Mazinaw area was quite bare. The land had been stripped of most of its trees Fire had consumed much of the already thin soil. At times, the slash left behind by the lumbering burned almost without restraint in a wall of fire that sometimes reached a height of almost four metres. Indeed, Vennachar, the settlement between the head of the lake and Denbigh, which once had boasted of two cheese factories, was completely destroyed by fire in 1903. No record of one big fire engulfing the whole area exists. Rather it was a series of smaller fires, spread over a number of years, that did the damage. For years, the hills looked bald with the charred stumps of the large pines still visible. While younger forest did return, the soil was now even less fertile and more eroded than it had been prior to the lumbering.

The large logging operations now were starting to pull out. Had modern lumbering practices been used and fire prevention vigorously pursued, it may have been possible to have managed the original pine as a renewable resource, but such was not the mindset of the day. Ontario was still in a pioneering mode which looked at nature as something to be conquered and exploited, with little

The Vennacher House, serving the needs of the traveller in the late 1800s.
Courtesy Lennox and Addington County Museum.

thought for the future. Such a perspective meant that the economic
boom created by logging was to be short-lived. With the lumber
companies no longer available as a local market, farming, now
saddled with high transportation costs and depleted soil, ceased to
be a reliable livelihood.

Alternatives were sought. The railway had been opening up the
West, a place offering a far greater opportunity for the homesteader to
make a decent living for himself and his family. People started to leave,
either for the Canadian prairies or for the cities. A further exodus
occurred after 1900, as more settlers moved to the clay belts of
Northern Ontario. Many Mazinaw area farms were left abandoned,
their fields to be overrun with birch and poplar. Even today, while
walking in the woods by Highway 41, one can discover sections of old
split log fences, snaking across what appears always to have been forest.
In the late spring it is possible to come upon a clump of blooming lilac,
seemingly growing wild along the roadside. These shrubs are not
native to the area, but were planted by many of the early settlers. Often
these living reminders are all that remain of their early efforts.

Of course, not everyone left. But the economy of the region,
which had relied so heavily on lumbering and agriculture for 50
years, had been severely shaken. In 1881, Barrie township had 486

residents. Even by 1941, some 60 years later, the population, calculated at 451, had not fully recovered.

The local farms which remained in operation were often located on the better soil. These were diversified operations; in addition to producing the traditional hay, grains and vegetables, they also raised pigs, chickens and cattle. The Meeks' farm, at the south end of the Mazinaw, had a particularly good apple orchard. Cattle were allowed to roam over adjacent Crown Land, foraging in both the forest and more open areas. However, the fresh milk supply exceeded the local demand and the high transportation costs prohibited shipping to outside markets. Consequently, milk was used primarily for cheese production. One local cheese factory, just south of Cloyne, was owned by Joseph Wise.

Even though times became more difficult, a local sense of community persisted and life was not without its pleasures. Jane Weese, in 1898, was a four-year-old child living on her family's farm, one which took in much of the east side of the lower lake. In 1956, as a 60-year-old woman, she was asked to record her memories of those early days. Her letter can be found in the Pioneer Museum in Cloyne. Within her written description she talks about warm family ties and memorable events, including community dinners:

> *They were held in Benny's grove on the edge of town. It was a beautiful grove of pines and well-kept. The church members spent many hours over their stoves preparing the food. There were long tables set up in the grove and a stand and a platform, where local talent put on entertainment and all kinds of goodies [were] sold at the stand; oranges, bananas, peaches, pears, plums, and lemonade and all kinds of candy and homemade ice cream. The men would set up a fireplace and the women would cook meat, bake potatoes and vegetables and the tables would groan with the food, cake, pie, cookies, pickles of every kind. . . . The charge was 25 cents. . . . We would have races for the kids and all kinds of races for the older folk, including the race in a potato sack for the men and the one with two legs tied together. It was a day to remember for us.*[1]

At one time there were several farms on the Mazinaw at the end of Campbell Bay. This bay is named after a woman, who, after having been widowed, stayed on her farm and raised a family, doing much of the farm labour herself. Located on sand flats, the fields have now grown over and are covered with second growth poplar, birch and maple, many up to six metres in height.

Until the early 1950s, the Head family took cattle from Cloyne into fields behind Campbell Bay. They even had several old cars which they left there as well as a fire engine which had been taken back over the ice. The Sniders also took cattle to graze in fields on the far side of the lake in Snider Bay. According to Ted Snider, the cattle got so that they knew the way themselves.[2]

Life was becoming more civilized and with progress came a greater regulation of life in general, and of farm animals in particular. The passing of Bylaw No.1 for the Municipal Corporation of Kaladar, Angesea and Effingham on March 4, 1899 illustrates:

> *That no horses be allowed to run at large at any season;*
> *That all peaceable cattle be allowed to run at large, with the*
> *   exception of bulls and stags . . .*
> *That all sheep be allowed to run at large, with the exception of*
> *   rams, which shall not be allowed to run at large between the*
> *   months of July and December inclusive;*
> *That no Swine be allowed to run at large at any time of year;*
> *The owners of any of the above mentioned animals doing damage*
> *   to any person's crops or property by getting over a lawful fence*
> *   shall be responsible for all damages done, to be recovered with*
> *   cost upon conviction before any of Her Majesty's Justices of the*
> *   Peace in and for the Counties of Lennox and Addington.*

Moses Lessard – Clerk 353[3]

Over the years, work continued on the Addington Road. By 1902 the trip by wagon from Kaladar to Cloyne had been cut from eight hours down to two or three, depending on the state of the road. While this was a tremendous improvement, the road, in need of constant repair, was the subject of a number of petitions from local citizens to the Government. The following petition, penned in 1911, is but one example:

County Of Barrie

To his Honor The Lieutenant Governor, In Council of the Province of Ontario, November 17, 1911

Honorable Sir,

We the undersigned petitioners humbly showeth that the Addington Colonization Road between Kaladar Station and the head of Massanaga Lake, some twenty-five miles in distance is in a very bad state of repairs.

Most of the road being very sparsely settled, it is impossible for the settlers to keep the road in possible condition. Owing to the large traffic from Cloyne and Denbigh to Kaladar Station and as it is the main road for all travel to the northern part of Addington County, and there are several mines in the locality some of them in operation and also a summer resort on the shores of Massanoga Lake near Cloyne. Therefore your petitioners humbly pray that your Honourable Minister of Public Works will grant the sum of fifteen hundred dollars $1500 to put said road in a possible condition and as in duty bound your petitioners will ever pray.[4]

Among the signatories to this petition were the names of men whose family names are still very familiar in the area. Included were: H. Bishop, William Head, James Wise, Charles Spencer, Elgin Brown, George Bishop, Ed Cummings, Robert Lacey, C. McGregor, William McCausland, John Thompson, Timothy Hunt, Joe Perry, B.H. Snider, D. Wedgwick, William Wise, S. Cuddy, J.N. Benny, C.L.

View of the Addington Road, just north of Kaladar in 1928. Courtesy Lennox and Addington County Museum.

Storey, Bert Hawley and W.C. Salmond. Also a signatory was Flora MacDonald Denison's husband, Howard. This would have been signed during the brief period in which he managed the Bon Echo Inn before their divorce in 1913. Despite periodic upgrades, by 1925 the trip from Kaladar to Cloyne, a distance of only 24 kilometres still took about one and three quarter hours.

Slowly, but persistently tourism slowly took stronger root as a source of economic activity. The Bon Echo Inn, constructed by Weston Price in 1899, provided employment for a few people and became a market for local produce. Fishing and hunting also lured more and more annual visitors. Reports of fishing on the lake in the 1920s indicate that it was not uncommon for two men to catch 40 pounds of fish in several hours. The Browns who lived at the head of the lake, were among the early farming families to recognize the potential of tourism, and took the initiative of establishing a campground on their farmland which continues to this day.

Dr. Morden, a regular hunter and visitor to the area from Kingston, rides the local stage, circa 1920. Courtesy Lennox and Addington County Museum.

The Northbrook Tourist Hotel, circa 1929. A dentist held clinics once a week in the dining room. Courtesy Lennox and Addington County Museum.

Fishing gradually increased the number of seasonal visitors. Courtesy Ministry of Natural Resources *(BE.4B-e).*

During earlier times, blueberries were often a vital part of a family's summer food supply and were gathered for winter use.

From the time that tourists began making their annual pilgrimage to the Mazinaw area, there have been stands at the side of the road loaded with blueberries and blueberry baking for sale. While there are areas in Northern Ontario which may have more extensive blueberry habitat, there are few regions this far south that can make that claim. For some, it seems that the world is divided by inclination into two groups; pickers and non-pickers. Today, for the former group, blueberry picking is still a tradition enjoyed by year-round residents and seasonal visitors alike.

In 1933, Highway 7 was opened as a provincial highway and work was begun on Highway 41, formerly known as the Addington Road. Mary Johnston reported from Cloyne in the December 1933 issue of the *Tweed News:*

> *Cloyne has taken on new life. One theme is on everyone's tongue; "We have a new highway." At last rumours and hearsay have crystallized into action and now we have the fact on the way. Camps for housing*

The recently completed Highway 41 opened up the area to hordes of blueberry pickers. Thomas Tyner made the trip annually with his neighbours, circa 1940.
Courtesy Lennox and Addington County Museum.

workmen are being built above Cloyne; Camp Frontenac at Mazinaw; Eagle Hill Camp and Matawatchan. . . . For weeks trucks have been hauling provisions and camp fittings. But in spite of abundance of work, the fly in the ointment is the meager wages of $10.00 and board per month.

Highway 41 was completed after two more years of construction, in 1935.

Four years later, electricity was welcomed into the region with much enthusiasm. Now local homes could be lit with something other than kerosene lamps; modern household appliances were purchased and local businesses could operate electrical machinery without resorting to the use of gas-burning generators. It was at this time that the large Hydro towers which cross Highway 41, south of Cloyne, were built. A tent camp was constructed and some local men were hired to augment Ontario Hydro's permanent construction crews. Once the path was cut through the bush, the towers were erected. Stringing the early lines was a daunting task. Teams of horses hauling the giant spools of wire worked some distance ahead of the main crew. From that time on, the daily lives of people were changed forever.

While diminished, the lumber trade had not vanished, but had altered. From the 1900s on, logging has focused on species other than

Shantymen, the Mazinaw area 1920. Courtesy Lennox and Addington County Museum.

pine. At one time there was a lumber camp located at the northeast end of Bon Echo Lake, just east of the mouth of Bon Echo Creek. In 1941, the Wells Bros. of Marmora lumbered maple, hemlock, yellow birch and black oak. From a camp on the northeast end of Kishkebus Lake, they transported the logs overland to German Bay and also down Shabomeka Lake, through Semicircle Lake into Mazinaw. Their lumber mill, located on the lower lake near where Holiday Haven is now, was later moved to a location just south of Highway 506 between Cloyne and Northbrook.

The largest of this past century's logging operations were those of the Sawyer-Stoll Lumber Company. In 1938, this Michigan-based firm acquired the timber rights to a large portion of Effingham township and appointed Wallace Johnston as General Manager to establish its operations in the region. On the shores of Stoll Lake, just to the north of the Mazinaw, the firm built an extensive mill and village, complete with company office, store, three bunk houses, staff houses and 12 cabins for mill hands and their families. There was also a recreational hall were staff enjoyed games of pool, movies and dances. At the height of its operations, the firm employed 200 workers who were paid 8 to 10 dollars a day. In 1942 the company added a school and a post office. The site was called Massanoga, the name formerly used for

Teams were used in the bush because of their versatility. Courtesy Tweed
Heritage Centre.

Mazinaw Lake. The milling operations consisted of the sawmill, a
boiler room, blacksmith's shop, barns and a planing mill.

The planing mill was moved in 1945 to Kaladar where it could
also dress the lumber shipped in by rail from the company's other
operations in Renfrew County. Under Johnston's direction, the
firm took over the local operations of the Wells Bros. and T.A.
Wilson lumber companies. By the mid-nineteen fifties, however, the
economics of Canada's lumbering industry had changed. Now the
Ontario industry was challenged by cheaper lumber being shipped
in by rail from the huge lumbering operations in British Columbia.
By 1958, the company was forced to sell its property in Kaladar and
consolidate its operations in Tweed. Four years later, Sawyer-Stoll
closed their Massanoga mill. Several years later, a partial recovery in
the Ontario market saw the start up of operations again but in 1975
a fire destroyed the original mill. It was replaced by a portable mill
for a few years, but eventually the operation was relocated in
Eganville to the north where the firm had purchased timber rights.[5]

Wallace Johnston died in 1958. His family, however, have never lost
connection with the region and still have a cottage on the lower lake.

Sleighs used to haul logs to the lake to await spring breakup. Courtesy Tweed Heritage Centre.

Log sleighs on the Mazinaw. Courtesy Tweed Heritage Centre.

By 1940 the Mazinaw area finally had become an integrated part of Southern Ontario. It had taken 85 years, from the time the first settlers homesteaded along the Addington Road in 1855, to move out of a condition of remoteness and inaccessibility. It would take another ten years, however, before tourism would reach its potential as the engine driving the local economy.

Sawyer-Stoll mill on Stoll Lake just to the north of the Mazinaw. Courtesy Tweed Heritage Centre.

MINING: AN UNFULFILLED HOPE

1850	Horatio Yates discovers a significant marble deposit in Barrie Township, but the site was never developed because of its remote location
1887	Golden Fleece Mine near Flinton is the first of the gold mines to be developed
1903	Star of The East Gold Mine opens
1909	Ore Chimney Mine near Northbrook — largest of the local mines
1934	Kaladar Marble Quarry in operation
1936	Accident takes the lives of 3 men at the Rich Rock Gold Mine near Flinton
1943	Mica Mine opens at the head of the Mazinaw. Mica is transported to Tweed for shipment to Europe
1980s	Last of the test drilling discontinued

CHAPTER 6

Mining: An Unfulfilled Hope

Since the turn of the century mining has occurred intermittently in the Mazinaw area. As logging activity declined, local residents, in their search for a possible replacement, hoped that mining would provide the needed economic stability. Promising surface deposits encouraged further exploration and, in some cases, even excavation and production. None of these efforts, however, has found sufficient quantities of quality ore to be viable for any length of time.

In 1850, Horatio Yates believed that he had found a significant deposit of marble at a site deep in the bush, north of Barrie township and six to eight kilometres east of Mazinaw. To this day, it has never been quarried, its remote location making the proposition uneconomic.

The Bey Mine, later called the Ore Chimney Mine, was located near Northbrook, where the power lines now cross the Harlowe Road. This, the largest mining operation in the area, was discovered by a local resident of Aboriginal descent, Johnny Bey. The mine operated intermittently from 1909 to 1936, with the level of activity depending on the price of gold. While the main shaft was excavated to a depth of 150 metres, the mine also had shafts extending at four

Shaft head, with managers and crew. Courtesy Pioneer Museum of Cloyne.

levels, all approximately of the same length. Employing over eighty men at the peak of its production, the mine site contained a number of buildings, including an office, a bunk house and a mill with 20 stamping machines which were used to grind the ore. A large cement dam approximately 18 metres long and 9 metres high was constructed at the end of Slave Lake (a small lake on the Skootamatta River between Cloyne and Northbrook). Its purpose was to generate power for the mine. Alas, this was not to continue. Presently owned by Albert Banner of Northbrook, the site is now inactive.

Another gold mine named the Golden Fleece, located closer to Flinton, started and stopped operation a number of times between 1887 and 1939. The site had several pits, a 24 metre shaft and an inclined 160 metre shaft as well as lateral tunnelling of about three-and-a-half kilometres. A 10-stamp milling machine, a diesel shop and living quarters for the workmen were erected, but none of these remains today.

Interior photograph of mining machinery. Courtesy Pioneer Museum of Cloyne.

A common pattern of early excitement and intense activity only to be followed by disappointment marked all of these efforts. The Star Of The East Gold Mine, located just off the Head Road to the south of the Mazinaw, was no exception. A reporter with the *Tweed News* filed the following report after visiting the site in 1905:

> *The mine was discovered by E. J. Cowain and has been in operation for about 2 years. For delightful situation and economic operation it is doubtful if it could be excelled. On one side is Lake McCausland, some 35 feet higher than the stamp mill and boarding house, and on the other side is Marble Lake, hundreds of feet below. A visit was made to the main shaft, which is sunk 180 feet in the solid rock down which the [Tweed] "News" man went on a vertical ladder nearly one hundred feet. Here he found a number of men busily engaged with steam drills getting out the valuable ore, which is then taken out in*

*large buckets by a steam hoist. There are drifts from the main shaft,
each some forty to fifty feet in length. . . .*

*A visit was next made to the boarding house for dinner. This is
a three storey structure with a basement containing bathrooms and
washrooms for the men. . . . Beside the boarding house there are three
residences, a large stable, and a barn. Along one side of the boarding
house is the office and just beyond is the stamp mill, a visit to which
was made after supper.*

*This was one of the most interesting parts. It is situated on the
side of a steep precipice overlooking Marble Lake, the advantage of this
being that the waste material requires handling but finds its own way
to the flat many feet below. At present, there is a ten stamp mill in operation which is kept busy from morning until night. There is also a blacksmith's shop. About 30 men are employed altogether on the property.*

*The arrangement for supplying the various buildings with water
is excellent. Pipes have been laid from McCausland Lake which is
supplied by springs connecting with all the buildings and the natural
pressure from the lake, on account of its elevation, is all that is
required.*

*An enormous sum of money has been expended on the prop-
erty and it is to be hoped that the enterprise shown by the company
will be amply rewarded. . . . The mine is, from all appearances, an
ideal one and the "News" wishes it every success.*[1]

The Star of The East Gold Mine no longer exists. Its main shaft
is now filled in and no buildings remain. In active operation for only
four years, between 1903 and 1907, the mine continued sporadically,
but was shut down permanently in 1935. One hundred tons of ore
were milled, but only several thousand dollars worth of gold were
ever recovered. Another gold mine, the Big Dipper Mine was a
smaller operation located just northeast of the Star of the East. Its
production was also short lived.

Work in the mines was dirty and dangerous. Using steam-driven
equipment and explosives, the men faced the hazards of cave-ins and

flooding, as well as steam burns, falls and explosions as they sunk shafts and cut lateral tunnels further and further into the rock. One of the worst tragedies was reported in the April 2nd, 1936 edition of the *Tweed News*:

Flinton – This community was shocked on Friday morning to hear of the terrible tragedy at the Rich Rock Gold Mine where three men lost their lives and six others narrowly escaped death from suffocation caused by a dynamite explosion in the shaft. All men were working the night shift at the mine and had just started duty when the explosion occurred at 2:30 am. The direct cause remains unknown. The bereaved widows, children and friends have the sympathy of the entire community.

Prospecting remained an active pursuit up until the late 1930s. Many of these men were amateurs who expended great energy in chasing their dream by means of claim striking and deal-making. The Oct. 8, 1936 edition of the *Tweed News* enthusiastically recounts the story of one of the more promising strikes.

The background of this strike really started in the early spring of 1930 when Mr. M. N. Marston pitched camp on the property of Henry Armstrong, adjoining the Bey Mines, at this small exciting village of Northbrook. He found the village very convenient for supplies, telephone services and Kaladar Station and Highway 7 close at hand. He found no time to be idle as the mosquito season was in full bloom.

Working quietly along the vein between the Bey and Rich Rock Mines, he staked properties. Following the vein east to Harlow, he met one of the country's most progressive men, M. Ed Morley who is now Game Warden. Mr. and Mrs. Morley had just suffered the loss of their home and store by fire and were living in a tent while clearing away the debris. Mr. Marston approached Morley regarding property to stake for prospecting. Mr. Morley at once signed a contract on his 400 acres, receiving 10% interest if gold is ever found.

At one time mine shafts were a familiar sight in the Mazinaw region.
Courtesy Ministry of Natural Resources.

Marston did find gold but, like so many other finds, it proved not to be in sufficient quantity.

The Kaladar Marble Quarry, located just south of Kaladar, consisted of two small open quarries, 1.2 kilometres apart. These were worked briefly in the mid 1930s, but also did not remain a viable operation. Evidence of the use of marble locally may be found at Actinolite United Church. According to the Provincial Plaque erected in front of the building, this church may be the only one in Canada with a completely marble exterior.

In the early 1940s, a mica mine with deposits which stretched over 40 hectares (100 acres) was worked just to the west of the head of the Mazinaw. The ore was trucked to Tweed for processing and much of it was then shipped in barrels to Europe. Although it was of high grade, the market was limited. Mica was used for such purposes as car and stove windows, but the later use of glass and plastics made it obsolete.

While test drilling remained a common occurrence up until the mid-1980s, currently no mine is in operation in the area. Geological mapping indicates, however, that the region contains scattered deposits of a number of minerals including copper, iron, mica, zinc, silver and gold. With advances in extraction technology, who knows what the future may hold.

BON ECHO INN: THE PRICES
AND THE DENISONS

1890s	• Well-to-do Americans discovering Southern Ontario as vacation area
	• Weston Price camps on shores of Weese farm in summers
1899	Bon Echo Inn built by Weston Price
1901	Inn completed: five cottages, staff house, tent platforms, services buildings, boat house, 9 metre water tower, two large docks
1910	Inn sold to Flora MacDonald Denison (suffragette, spiritualist and supporter of the arts)
1916 – 1920	• Publication of arts newsletter – *Sunset Of Bon Echo*,
	• formation of the Whitman Club of Bon Echo in honour of the American poet
1916 – 1929	Association with Group of Seven who came to paint at Bon Echo
1919	Carving of "Old Walt" inscription dedicated to Walt Whitman
1921	Flora MacDonald Denison dies. Management of hotel taken over by her son Merrill (author and one of Canada's first playwrights)

1922	Inn has horses, tennis courts, outdoor stage for theatrical events
1926	Inn has staff of 40 and guest list of over 200
1927	Newspaper articles by Denison critical of government's actions regarding conservation and plight of farmers of the Canadian Shield
1929	Business hit by depression. Inn is closed and rented out
1936	Fire destroys hotel – loss only partially covered by insurance
1950s	Committee struck to turn Bon Echo into training/conference centre
1958	Merrill Denison donates lands to Province
1965	Bon Echo Provincial Park officially opens

CHAPTER 7

Bon Echo Inn: The Prices and the Denisons

The Bon Echo Inn was constructed on the peninsula across from the Rock in 1899, built by a young man by the name of Weston Price who had grown up in Newburg, just north of Napanee. As a university student, he had camped in the summers on the Weese farm, located on the lower Mazinaw. At the time he was studying dentistry in Cleveland, but, once established in practice, he married a young woman from home. They came to the Mazinaw to spend their honeymoon camping. Having taught school in nearby Ardoch, she was familiar with the general area. It was while on their honeymoon that they decided to buy the point of land opposite the Rock from the Weese family and also to acquire land from the Tappings just to the north. Their intent was to build lodgings where like-minded naturalists could enjoy Bon Echo. Weston continued, however, to practise dentistry in Cleveland.

It must have taken a great deal of faith to believe that such a venture would be successful, given the remote location. There were, however, a number of factors working in their favour. By 1900, the Americans had discovered Ontario. Both the Thousand Islands and the Rideau area became favourite cottage spots and the Kawarthas,

*Weston Price - American
Dental Association photograph.*
Courtesy Ministry of
Natural Resources.

Muskokas and Georgian Bay were emerging as desirable holiday des-
tinations. It was quite fashionable for the well-to-do to vacation at
resort hotels, many of which were accessible only by train. The
CPR line through Kaladar, just recently completed, made the
proposition of building a hotel a more realistic one.

The fact that Price was able to prepare the site and build the hotel
in only a year and a half is testament to his determination. Since a
fire had swept the point at the Narrows ten years before, the site first
had to be cleared of the charred remains. Erosion was also a problem.
The water level had been raised about 1.2 metres in the late 1800s to
accommodate the needs of lumbering and the property had experienced significant erosion. Many of the logs remaining along the
shore and on the property were used to build up the banks to prevent
further damage. Ultimately, slightly over 900 metres of retaining wall
were built. Other logs left from lumbering were sawn into boards and
used in the construction of the buildings. A portable sawmill, brought
in for this purpose, produced between 23,000 and 30,500 metres of
the needed lumber. With all of the buildings made of unfinished

boards, except for the hotel itself which was built of lumber which had been dressed on one side, a very rustic look was established.

The Inn, designed by Cleveland architect Charles E. Tousley, was not a simple task to build. All supplies had to be brought in by wagon along the Addington Colonization Road. Price, fortunately, had the help of local people, many of whom were skilled carpenters or jacks-of-all-trades eager for paid work. This labour was not expensive. Unskilled workers were paid a dollar a day and experienced carpenters a dollar and a half. Unfortunately, partway through the construction, disaster struck when the north wall, which had not been properly braced, was toppled in a wind storm. With nails being so very expensive and not available locally, many hours were spent in removing nails from the broken lumber and straightening them for reuse.

Despite these hardships, by 1901, a number of buildings had been completed. A three-storey frame hotel completely encircled with veranda, five cottages, a staff house, tent platforms, service buildings, a boat house, a nine metre water tower and two large docks (one on each side of the Narrows) were all standing. The interior of the hotel's main floor was lined with birch and elm bark to give a natural appearance. A windmill was used for power, and the first telephone line in the area was strung to Kaladar Station.

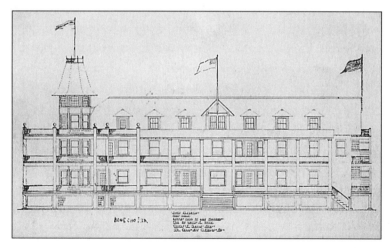

Drawing of Bon Echo Inn before construction. Courtesy Pioneer Museum of Cloyne.

Water recreation was, of course, a prime attraction for the fledgeling tourist operation. Weston Price purchased 25 rowboats, a number of canoes and fourteen small launches with inboard motors. These one-cylinder, Palmer Bros. gas engines were one of the first internal combustion engines to be produced for pleasure boats. Decorative as well as practical canvas tops edged with a fringe provided shade for the passengers. A diving platform, constructed just

The Inn as it appeared in the off-season. Note the water tower at far right. Courtesy Friends of Bon Echo Park.

The rotunda at the Inn. Courtesy Ministry of Natural Resources.

Note the American flag at the stern of the boat, a reflection of the number of visitors from the United States. Courtesy Ministry of Natural Resources.

above the Narrows at the face of the Rock, proved to be a favourite with the more energetic guests.

Access to Bon Echo was by means of a foot bridge constructed over the Narrows, and by a set of metal stairs going up the almost sheer face of the Rock. Often, guests would have a box lunch packed to take with them as they climbed the steep stairs to the top. Once there, they enjoyed the view and often picked blueberries. A number of local people who also picked blueberries either for sale or for their own use, frequently made use of this stairway. Eventually, it was damaged by ice and finally taken down in 1940, long after the demise of the hotel.

In 1906, the rates at the Inn ranged from nine to fifteen dollars per week, a rate considered relatively steep for the period. Advertising brochures refer to Mazinaw by its earlier name of Massanoga, and encourage tourists to take the Canadian Pacific Railway to Kaladar Station, travel by coach to the foot of the lake, then complete their journey by boat on the *Wanderer*. Written accounts of the ride from Kaladar describe the bald mountains covered with white weathered stumps, left from the pine forest decimated earlier by the lumbering.

The bridge over the Narrows gave access to the Rock. Courtesy Pioneer Museum of Cloyne.

Diving platform immediately adjacent to the Rock. Courtesy Ministry of Natural Resources (BE.4A-e).

The Prices were an interesting couple. Strict Methodists, they attracted similarly-minded guests. No liquor was allowed and "quiet Sundays" were observed, with religious services held at the hotel. Merrill Denison's boyhood recollection of Weston Price was that of a thin and very active man. Price was knowledgeable about mechanical things and could fix most problems himself.

According to Denison, it was Mrs. Price who named the cliff Bon Echo. Prior to the Prices acquisition, it had been called the Massanoga Rock. Then, the reverberating echo was a much more dramatic and distinguishing feature at the turn of the century than it is today. At that time the second growth forest was significantly less dense and the surrounding rock was thus more exposed.

After a decade of successful operation, the Prices sold the Inn. Their only son, Donald, was ill at the time and was later to die of spinal meningitis. Following the sale to the Denisons, they devoted their summers to providing dental care to children in underdeveloped countries. In doing so, Price noticed that what people in various cultures ate had an effect on the number of cavities they had. This observation led to more formal studies and, ultimately, to the publication of these findings. At his death, years later, full page obituaries appeared in leading American dental journals, documenting his contribution to dental research. It is interesting, though, to note that the obituaries make no mention of Price's connection with Mazinaw.

Flora MacDonald Denison and her husband Howard acquired the property in 1910. The Massanoga Rock, however, had been a legend in the Denison family for some time. Flora's son, Merrill, told the story of his grandfather hearing of a "mysterious and awe inspiring cliff on the Mishinog, located somewhere in the dark reaches of the forest to the north."[1] The grandfather had been involved in the logging indus-

Flora and a young Merrill Denison. Courtesy Ministry of Natural Resources (BE.4A - a).

try along the Skootamatta River and later travelled to the Mazinaw in the 1870s, where he claimed to have discovered the cave which Myers had found 50 years before. When he returned three years later, he could not find it again. Fire had obliterated all signs of recognition of the location. A skeptic, of course, might ask why, if he had discovered a silver mine, it would have taken him three years to return? What is known is that the Denisons first visited the Inn in 1901. Flora and Howard had talked to Weston Price about purchasing a cottage lot on the property, but he was reluctant to sell. Instead, the Denisons bought a lot just to the south and had a cottage on the lake for nine years before purchasing the hotel for fifteen thousand dollars.[2]

Flora's early years of life were not easy. Her father, the Principal of the Picton Grammar School, had quit this secure position to go into partnership in a mining venture with Billa Flint, the Belleville-based lumber baron. Her father's money quickly ran out and the family had to make do with very little. Having to leave school at 15 years of age, Flora taught in a one-room schoolhouse in the French Settlement, near Flinton, before moving to Toronto where she became a seamstress.

Her twenties and thirties were busy years. In the late 1880s, she moved to Detroit and wrote for the *Detroit Free Press*. It was there in 1892 that she met, and married, Howard Denison. The couple moved back to Toronto and Flora joined the staff of Simpsons, where she soon became manager of the store's custom-made dress department. Later, Flora started her own successful dress business and continued her writing on a part-time basis. She was responsible for a "labour" page in the *Toronto Sunday World* and contributed to *Saturday Night Magazine*. Her strong views on the plight of working women, particularly of those in the garment industry, won her recognition among the members of Canada's Suffragette movement. In 1912, they elected Flora as President. In that capacity, she attended an International Suffrage Alliance Conference in Budapest and conducted a speaking tour across Europe.

The Denison's marriage was not a close one. Howard Denison sold merchandise to the lumbering camps and was away much of the time. Following the purchase of the Inn, he managed the operation for the first two years of their ownership before the marriage ended in divorce in 1913.

Flora, however, was a resourceful woman. The year 1914 saw her working as a seamstress in Napanee during the off-season, earning money for her son's education. In 1916, she spent the winter months on the lecture circuit, as a paid speaker for the New York Women's Suffrage campaign.

Although Flora never had the opportunity to attend university, she developed a love of the arts. She published a short semi-autobiographical novel called *Mary Melville, The Psychic*, a book based on her elder sister's extraordinary psychic powers. This affinity for the spiritual, led her to explore the tenets of Theosophy, the encouragement of free thought in search of truth. During the years 1916 to 1920, she published a newsletter called *The Sunset of Bon Echo* which was both an arts publication and advertising for the hotel.

A Bon Echo brochure produced in 1911 describes activities at the Inn: "Teachers, artists and lecturers will find the atmosphere of Bon

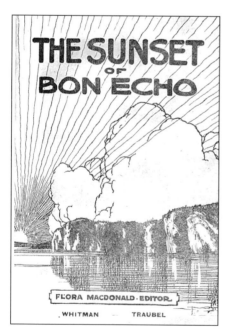

The literary magazine of the Bon Echo Inn. Courtesy Pioneer Museum of Cloyne

Brochures advertising the Bon Echo Inn. Courtesy Pioneer Museum of Cloyne (left) and Ministry of Natural Resources (BE4A-C) (right).

Echo one in which liberal minds will be invited to express their noblest and best, and classes along artistic and progressive lines will be welcomed ... music, dancing, games, contests on land and water and exploring excursions will be encouraged."[3]

From 1913 to the late 1920s, the Inn became a centre for visitors interested in painting, theatre and the arts. Authors James Thurber and Morley Callaghan, among others, were welcome visitors. Another person of international fame, Frank Lloyd Wright suggested plans for the expansion of Bon Echo, but these proved to be too expensive for the Denisons.

Flora was particularly taken with the democratic ideals of the American poet, Walt Whitman, and founded "The Whitman Club" at Bon Echo in his honour. During the years covering the First World War, Flora's interest in Whitman's poetry grew until it took on mystical connotations. She saw in this poet a spokesperson for the ideals of freedom, equality and democracy. While the poet had died in 1892 and, thus, never visited Bon Echo, Flora corresponded on a regular basis with his official biographer, Horace Traubel of New York. He soon became a frequent visitor. Traubel would die at Bon Echo two weeks after the dedication of the "Old Walt" inscription in August of 1919. It would not be until the following summer that the actual inscription was cut into the Rock.[4]

Originally, Flora wanted a bust of Walt Whitman carved into the Rock, similar to the busts of the U.S. presidents, done later at Mount Rushmore in the United States by Guzton Borglum. She commissioned a well-known Toronto sculptor, Jack Banks, to make a quarter-scale model, but this venture also proved to be too costly.[5] Today, such an idea does not fit with notions of environmental conservation and would be considered a desecration. In its day, however, such projects were very much accepted.

Upon Merrill Denison's return from the war in 1919, he learned of his mother's plans for the inscription honouring Whitman. Being an architect by training, he readily agreed to complete the working drawings. The passage used was taken from Walt Whitman's "Song of Myself" in the book *Leaves of Grass* and reads as shown:

OLD WALT
1819 – 1919
Dedicated to the Democratic Ideals of
Walt Whitman
by
Horace Traubel and Flora MacDonald
"My foothold is tenon'd and mortised in granite
I laugh at what you call dissolution
And I know the amplitude of time"

Whitman asserted the belief that we learn naturally by living, and that our knowledge grows through a series of lives, over a long period of time. His poetry celebrated personal freedom and the brotherhood of mankind. At the rededication of the Old Walt inscription on June 29, 1965, Merrill said of his mother that: "She saw in the qualities of the Big Rock – elemental, seemingly ageless, so little affected by the passage of the centuries – the self-same qualities she found in Whitman: the poet and the man."[6]

The task of chiseling the inscription was not an easy one. A local miner, by the name of Sol Cummings, was hired to drill three holes into the Rock, high above the water's surface, and to insert three iron pins with eyes at the end. This was completed in the winter as he stood on a ladder when the lake was frozen. The next summer, a large scaffold was constructed and suspended by block and tackle from the iron pins, providing a platform on which the stone cutters could operate. A large raft was used to ferry supplies and to provide an additional working area. Two stonemasons from Aberdeen, Scotland, were hired to do the work. Starting in June, and working only with hand tools, it took them all summer to complete the inscription. The rock surface was so hard that they had to stop frequently to sharpen their chisels on a portable hand forge which had been affixed to the raft.

Two years later, in May of 1921, Flora MacDonald Denison unexpectedly died of pneumonia at the age of 54. She left the Inn and all of its property to her son Merrill. As the relationship between mother and son had been very close, her sudden illness and death came as a great shock and was a difficult adjustment for Merrill.

Merrill Denison was trained as an architect, having studied at Columbia University, the École des Beaux Arts in Paris and at the University of Toronto. It was while he was in Toronto, however, that he decided to forgo architecture and follow his love of the theatre. During his tenure as director of the Hart House Theatre, he quickly developed a reputation as an up-and-coming talent. He is now recognized as having been a leading Canadian playwright and author. During his career he wrote 26 radio plays and a number of stage productions. His radio play, *On Christmas Night*, was the curtain raiser for the first Metropolitan Opera Broadcast ever made on NBC. His book, *Klondike Mike*, the biography of Mike Mahoney, the man who started the Klondike Gold Rush, made the best-seller list. Denison also wrote a number of corporate histories, including those for Massey-Harris, the Bank of Montreal, Molsons, Ontario Hydro and the American Auto Industry. As well, he was a contributor to ten different magazines and wrote articles for the *Toronto Star*.

An arts enthusiast, Merrill met the members of the Group of Seven at the Arts And Letters Club in Toronto. This organization was a musical, theatrical and academic society which used the talents of local painters to assist with set design and the advertisements for its stage productions. The Club exists to this day. Merrill's friendship with the group deepened when some of its members assisted as set consultants on the production of Merrill's plays, *Brothers-in-Arms* (1921), *From Their Own Place* (1922) and *The Weather Breeder* (1924), all of which were produced at the Hart House Theatre.

As a consequence of this relationship, most of the Group of Seven, including Frank Johnston, Arthur Lismer, A.Y. Jackson, Franklin Carmichael and A.J. Casson, visited Bon Echo and painted the Rock, as did other prominent artists, such as Charles Comfort and Will Ogilvie. Carmichael, Jackson and Johnston also did commercial work for the Inn. It was Frank (Franz) Johnston who painted the masthead for Flora's literary newsletter, *Sunset Of Bon Echo,* in 1916. In 1928, Merrill asked A.J. Casson and Franklin Carmichael to paint a series of black and white oil sketches of the Rock to use for advertisements. Each completed approximately ten paintings.

Many of the Group's paintings can be seen at the McMichael Canadian Art Collection in Kleinburg, the National Gallery of Canada in Ottawa, the Art Gallery of Ontario in Toronto and at the Agnes Etherington Art Centre in Kingston. At the McMichael Gallery are several brochures on the Bon Echo Inn, illustrated by A.Y. Jackson. One is very striking, showing a red and blue rock on a blue lake and a deep red reflection in the water with a lighter blue sky.

Over the years, the Rock has attracted a number of other artists who have tried to capture its spirit and power. The book, *Massanoga, The Art of Bon Echo* by Robert Stacey and Stan McMullin, chronicles and illustrates this body of work. It is not easy to reflect the many moods of the Rock as light and season dramatically alter its face. As well, each painter brings a unique perspective to the task. Stuart MacKinnon, in his memorable book of poems on the Mazinaw illustrates:

Algonkin for picture writing painting book:
first the Algonkin red ochre painters
then Flora's meeting place for painters
Bell-Smith's dark smoky red promontory
Jackson's glad red meeting place
Johnston's slashes of bright flame
against the jagged face
Comfort's idyll with humpy elephantine backs
Casson's cool high windy watercolour.
All came to stay and paint
but Carmichael saw it from the top
looking down across rock and lake
and point where the inn stood
all in twisting sinous flowing lines,
massive swirling energy of rock
within water within land.
There is no sky in his landscape,
only the original landforms
looking like they are in movement, and they are.[7]

Merrill divided his time between his writing career and the Inn. He continued his mother's encouragement of the arts at Bon Echo, staging outdoor theatrical events with guests taking leading roles. These were often spontaneous efforts based on the events of the day. In addition, Merrill and a number of his friends performed his plays at the Orange Lodge in Tweed with the proceeds going to the United Church women's group. His play, *The Weather Breeder*, was first performed there.[8] To honour his work and recognize his contributions, the Lodge building was restored as a Centennial project and renamed the Merrill Denison Playhouse.

During the 1920s, the Inn did well financially. As a source of employment for a number of local residents and a consumer of local supplies Bon Echo Inn contributed much to the local economy. The Meek's farm supplied the hotel with milk, eggs, vegetables, cheese and meat, while apples came from a number of local orchards. In 1922, a riding stable, and tennis and badminton courts were added. By 1926, the Inn had a guest list of over 200 people. A staff of forty were employed in a variety of tasks from providing meals, to cleaning rooms and doing laundry. The grounds had to be kept orderly, the vegetable gardens maintained, wood supplied and the boats and buildings kept in good repair. In the off-season, things were closed up, a job in itself. Winter activities were limited to general caretaking and the cutting of ice blocks for use the next summer.

Merrill's first wife, Muriel Goggin, was a woman ten years younger than himself, whom he had met at Hart House. Also an author, she wrote under the pen name of Frances Newton. Using her childhood experiences in the North West Territories, she wrote the girl's novel *Susannah of the Mounties* and its sequels. This book was made into a movie starring Shirley Temple, and was a considerable success. Muriel managed the Bon Echo Inn, even before they were married in 1926, and continued until ill health made this impossible.

Greystones, now used to house the Friends of Bon Echo gift shop, originally was built as a schoolhouse in Campbell Bay. In 1924, it was moved to the Park, to be used as a cottage. Guests who stayed there included many of the Group of Seven, Yousuf Karsh, the world famous portrait photographer then living in Ottawa, and W.O. Mitchell, the author of a number of well-known books and plays including *Who Has Seen the Wind*. Dollywood, now the Park's

Visitor Centre, was one of several other cottages built in conjunction with the Inn. This particular one was constructed for the Proctor family of Toronto and named after Mrs. Dolly Proctor.

A central theme of Denison's plays was the devastating effect that economic hardship can have on family life and on the human spirit. His play, *Marsh Hay*, based on a family who lived on the Loon Lake (Skootamatta) Road before World War I, received rave reviews when it was last performed at the Shaw Festival in Niagara-on-the-Lake in 1996. Other plays in the collection, *The Unheroic North*, also reflected the lives of individuals from the Mazinaw area.

Denison was very critical of the government's former colonization roads and free land grant programs, believing that such ventures had been in error. From his perspective, this negative legacy included poverty, abandoned farms, poor roads and acres of burnt forest lands. He was also appalled at what he perceived to be an attitude of apathy and indifference on the part of those in power. People, many of whom had no farming background, had been encouraged with free land grants to settle and put down roots. While it was true that a number had moved on, others stayed, struggling to eke out an existence. Their children attended country schools for the primary and junior grades, but once they reached adolescence, they had to board in the nearest town or city to go to secondary school. This meant that children from the Mazinaw area had to attend school in Napanee. This type of social and economic hurdle discouraged many from getting the kind of academic background or trade skills required to prosper in an increasingly complex society, thus furthering their disadvantage. It was Denison's view that this perpetual cycle of hardship was caused not so much by the people affected, as by the fact that the area should never have been opened for agricultural settlement in the first place.

An an article dated February 19, 1927, in the *Toronto Star Weekly*, Denison expressed his support for the government's Forestry Act. The Act provided an opportunity for a number of subsistence farmers to move to more fertile areas of the province.

Gaunt farmsteads which tell a tragic tale of the futility of human struggle against nature will be abandoned. Roads, that are little better than overgrown paths through the wilderness, will be closed. Townships of which less than 10 percent is under cultivation or in which there are less than 25 settlers, will be taken back into the crown, and by it dedicated to the forest from which they never should have been taken.[9]

Merrill Denison also tried to awaken Ontarians to the fact that the Canadian Shield represented significant tourism potential, and that this industry could be a boon to communities which had always had to struggle economically. Even in that day, Eastern Ontario was within twenty-four-hours travel of 50,000,000 people. He encouraged the government to pursue fish hatcheries, good roads and game preserves as a means to promote tourism. A staunch advocate of reforestation and conservation, he pointed to such countries as Germany, Switzerland and France who, years earlier, had taken steps to reforest areas not suitable for agriculture. His articles in the *Toronto Star* won him the support of a number of professional foresters working for the Provincial Department of Lands and Forests who often visited Bon Echo to discuss issues of conservation. Through those associations Denison met, and later became friends with William Finlayson, the then Deputy Minister of the Department. In reality, Denison became an unpaid advisor.[10]

Even before the worst of the Depression, the resort business was experiencing difficult times and Merrill was forced to close the Inn to guests in late 1929. To help cover expenses, he leased it to an aviation training firm, the Leavens Brothers, which continued to operate the site as a summer hotel. Merrill now used the property as a rural estate and continued to do much of his writing there.

Like any region, the Mazinaw area was not without its "bad apples." Correspondence from the time indicates that whenever the caretaker, George Levere, had to be away from Bon Echo in the off season, Merrill worried that someone might break into the hotel. Because of its isolation, the property was very vulnerable. There was little police support and absolutely no fire protection. In 1933, Merrill pressed charges against several people for theft. While no one was convicted, Merrill hoped the publicity the trial received would act as a deterrent.[11]

His worst fears concerning fire were realized when the Inn and many of the buildings were destroyed in September of 1936. The fire started when lightning struck the bakehouse at two o'clock in the morning. Eyewitness accounts tell of how most of the hotel was consumed in an hour. Regrettably, the loss was only partially covered by insurance. At one time, there had been over thirty buildings, but now the property was no longer viable as a resort. Instead, Merrill rented the site from 1929 to 1934, for use as a boys' camp operated by Kenneth Ketchum who later became head-master of St. Andrew's College, and also to a beer company for the camping enjoyment of its employees. Throughout, the property remained his summer residence.

Mike Schwager was hired as a caretaker shortly after the fire, and stayed on the property until his death in 1974 at the age of 91. Mike was a gruff old bachelor who lived year round in his cabin on the Bon Echo property. A trusted employee, he served the Denisons in a reliable manner, doing the many odd jobs always in need of attention. He also ensured that trespassers were promptly informed of the fact that the property was out-of-bounds and were ushered off the site. Mike had been the chief carpenter when Skootamatta Lodge was built in the 1920s and, at that time, had lived on a small island in Skootamata Lake. He did many paintings of the Rock in a self-taught, rustic style and became a well-known local figure. Today, his artworks are valued as collectibles.[12]

In the summer of 1951, Mary Savigny started her employment with Merrill Denison, as his manuscript typist. Later, she would operate the several remaining cottages on the property as a summer resort. In 1997, she published a book on her experiences called *Bon Echo, The Denison Years*, a first-hand account providing valuable insights into the lives of the Denisons. In the book she describes Merrill as being:

... a slow moving man of medium height, somewhat overweight with a large head, dark complexion... deep brown eyes and a penetrating stare. . . . Always I was to be amazed at his child-like curiosity and eagerness to learn about something new – even something so mundane as cleaning a typewriter...He had a delightful sense of humour, with an even-tempered patience. He was a gentle man and I liked him.[13]

This positive view, however, was not shared by all. While there were a number of local residents who, through employment and other contact, established solid relationships with the Denisons, there remained a general suspicion and guardedness.

Mr. and Mrs. Denison were [seen as] summer people, a grumpy pair of authors who had no social connection with the village. No one dare set foot on the property. The gate at the highway was kept closed and if spotted, anyone approaching by boat would be sent away. . . . A more serious criticism was that Denison had not only offended the local people, but that he'd even made a lot of money from a book he had written which ridiculed the locals. That book was Boobs In The Woods, *sixteen hilarious sketches of Muriel's and Merrill's unique experiences as managers of their wilderness summer resort. In no way was it a put-down of the local people. The "Boobs" were Muriel and Merrill.*[14]

While people assumed the Denisons to be wealthy because of their land holdings and the success of Merrill's writings, such was not the case. Mary Savigny provides an example from 1953:

From time to time he [Merrill] produced a fistful of invoices and bills, invariably overdue. Mostly they were requests for membership fees from various authors' and historical associations, subscription notices from various magazines, insurance premiums and the dreaded $600-plus tax bill from Barrie township for the more than 1,600 acres Merrill and Muriel owned. Though he had five bank accounts; two in New York, two in Toronto and one in Tweed, there was rarely enough on hand to cover the indebtedness.[15]

Merrill Denison later in life. Courtesy Ministry of Natural Resources.

Being without an heir, Merrill needed to plan for the property's future use. In doing so, he was driven by his mother's intent that Mazinaw be a site from which worthwhile things for mankind would flow. Because of his own conservationist interests, he wanted to popularize the idea that the environment should be protected and used for socially constructive purposes. Merrill discussed, with William Finlayson, the possibility of the Province establishing a college for foresters and offered to donate Bon Echo as a site. In an elaborate brief, he argued for the many advantages which such a centre of study could provide. The government agreed in principle, and the plan was publicly announced and reported in the *Toronto Star*. A change of government caused a rethinking of the decision, however, and the centre was established at Dorset, south of Algonquin Park, where a forest ranger school had already been established.

Merrill next proposed that the property be developed as a meeting place for groups concerned with the betterment of democratic institutions: an opportunity for those of differing views to rub shoulders with one another. In the 1950s, a group was formed to turn Bon Echo into an adult education and conference centre. Representatives from John Labatt Ltd. and from a number of labour organizations were members on the committee. While several conferences were held at Mazinaw, the centre was never constructed because of insufficient financial support.

Merrill's wife, Muriel had first been diagnosed with Parkinson's Disease in 1942 and over the years became progressively more disabled. She died in 1954 after a lengthy illness. Three years later, Lisa Robert Andrews of Washington DC became the second Mrs. Denison.

In 1955, the province passed legislation enabling the Department of Lands and Forests to accept gifts and purchase, or expropriate, land for the establishment of provincial parks. The parks were to serve the purpose of promoting recreation, education and conservation. By the mid 1950s, the shoreline properties at Mazinaw had increased considerably in value. Good roads had cut the travelling time for cottagers, making the area more accessible and the property more valuable. While some smaller parcels of property from the original holding were sold, there is no doubt that Merrill Denison could have realized a considerable profit had he subdivided and sold all of his property as individual building lots. Instead, in 1959, he donated the land on both sides of the Narrows to the province for the purpose of forming a park. Bon Echo Provincial Park officially opened in 1965. A plaque erected at the Narrows was inscribed with a dedication of the parkland to his mother and his first wife Muriel.

Even after the Park's creation, Merrill kept the connection with Bon Echo. The agreement which he had struck with the Provincial Government allowed him to retain the remaining buildings, including Dollywood, for his personal use. In the summers which followed, he continued to use Mazinaw as a retreat and was more than pleased with the way in which the Park was being developed.

Merrill was now getting older, and as the years passed, his health deteriorated. On June 12, 1975, Merrill Denison died following a stroke, alone in a hospital in La Jolla, California. He was 81 years of age. Today, thousands of summer visitors are the beneficiaries of this man's most generous bequest.

RECENT HISTORY AND
THE GROWTH OF TOURISM

1940s	Tourism grows. Camp Mazinaw opens and several fishing-based tourist operations established
1950s and 60s	Parents of baby boomers buy cottage property
1956	First official climb of the face of Bon Echo
1965	Bon Echo Provincial Park opens
1971	First continuous school, teaching grades from one to OAC opened by Minister of Education in Cloyne
1980	Metal stairs installed to assist visitors to climb up to the top of Bon Echo
1997	Blueberry Jamboree featured on the CBC as an example of small town initiative
1998	Mazinaw enters cyberspace with Mazinaw On-line

CHAPTER 8

Recent History and the Growth of Tourism

Over the past fifty years the complexion of the lake has changed. The opening of Highway 401 and improvements to Highways 7 and 41 gradually increased accessibility for people from both Toronto and Ottawa. The trip from Toronto, that once took six hours along the old Highway 2 in the 1950s, has been reduced to three and a half. There are 330 cottages now on the lake and only 15 percent of the shoreline remains as Crown Land. Despite this increased popularity, Mazinaw is still relatively unspoiled. The fact that the region is some distance from large urban areas has allowed it to escape the worst aspects of overpopulation. Much of the lake's shoreline remains as it looked years ago, thanks to the parcels of remaining Crown Land and to regulations which now require new structures to be built 30 metres back from the water. While summer boat traffic can sometimes be a distraction, those who can visit in the off-season are transported back to a near-wilderness setting.

From its inception in 1940, Camp Mazinaw was advertised as a six-week camp for 60 young boys and was run as a successful business for 50 years before it was closed and the property sold. Located on the west side of the lower lake, the camp earned a first-rate reputation.Its founder was P.K. Hambly, a classics teacher and director of guidance at East York Collegiate in Toronto. He was joined by Harry Hull and C. R. (Blackie) Blackstock also of East York. Others involved, as time went on, included R. Rourke, Jim Smart and Paul McLean. Accommodation for the campers consisted of 12 cabins with meals being served in a central lodge. For a number of seasons, the camp cooks were Ida Meeks and Kay O'Brien, both of Cloyne. While activities included swimming, sailing and woodcraft, canoe tripping was its primary focus.

A highlight of the camp was its Grand Councils. Three were held every season and consisted of a decorated council ring, "Chiefs" in full traditional Native costume, reports from far-wandering scouts and tests of strength and skill. Such pageantry was just the thing for small boys. The camp hymn captures much of this spirt:

Dear land of Youth, on lips our praise is forming,
For paddles flashing smoothly in the sun:
For the brown thrust of Youth grown free and supple
While wind-blown waves caress the shore.

This is our land on which like wind we wander
Along white streams and lakes where mist arises.
Its here we dream as free as clouds adrifting,
Within our hearts a song of love.

We softly sing around the campfire's embers
While moon beams play in shadows of pine;
Contentment falls, then peace spreads o'er our sleep
In this our home with stars ashine.[1]

The camp's closing in the late 1980s was received with regret by many around the lake. The values it espoused of self reliance, comradeship and love of the outdoors were a part of what made it such a good neighbour.

Camp Mazinaw as it looked in the 1950s on the west side of the lower lake. Courtesy Mrs. H. Hull.

Meal time in the main lodge of Camp Mazinaw. Courtesy Mrs. H. Hull.

Waterfront activity at the Camp included swimming, water sports, canoeing and sailing. Courtesy Mrs. H. Hull.

By the late 1940s, there were a number of local businesses which had been established to serve the growing market for tourism. At the head of the Lake, Whippoorwill Lodge had cabins and a dining room for vacationers. A little further south, Fred Garbit established Popi Camp, the forerunner of what is now Bon Echo Villa. Fred was a well-respected and inventive man who had cabins for rent, and used a hand-driven pump to sell gas to those with outboard motors. Just to the south of this property was probably the most attractive of the resorts, called the Hermitage. It had beautiful pine floors and advertised fishing, hunting, swimming, boating and hiking. Open all year around, it had accommodation for 24 guests. Owned by an American, William Maloney, the resort ran into financial difficulty, closed in the late 40s, and was later destroyed by fire. The Mazinaw Inn, located on a beautiful sand beach at the south end of the lake, was another such enterprise. Established in 1948, it operated for 25 years as a resort and is now used as a children's camp. Each had fleets of small boats available for rent which were enthusiastically used by their guests on their early dawn and dusk trolling ventures.

While many a questionable story was told about the ones that got away, Ralph Frid, the younger son of the owner of the Mazinaw Inn still has the picture to prove that he is the only person in the history of the lake to ever have caught a smoking fish. This species is now extinct.

*Mazinaw Inn's fleet of flat
bottom fishing boats.*
Courtesy Ralph Frid.

Note the human-like teeth in this example of a Smoking Fish! Courtesy Ralph Frid.

During the 1950s and 60s, throughout Ontario, camping and cottaging gained in popularity, particularly among families with baby boom children. Mazinaw, like so many other lakes, became a summer playground for kids of all ages. Fishermen now had to compete for predominance. Increasingly, sailing, motor boats and water-skiing became the norm. John-Ross Hodgins, whose family had a cottage on the lower lake, was one of the more enthusiastic of this new breed. An excellent athlete, John taught himself to stand on his head on a chair, while being towed on a circular disk behind a boat. This stunt, along with his engaging personality, landed him a job as a clown in the Kirk Cove water ski show operated on nearby Big Gull Lake. Eventually, he would become one of the few Canadians to ever perform in Cypress Gardens, Florida as both a water ski jumper and kite flyer.

During these years, summers on the lake were largely pleasant, lazy and uneventful. Such was not the case, however, one sunny afternoon in 1953. Arnold Flieler, still resident in the area, had a plane in which he took tourists for sightseeing flights. His small business, Flieler's Skyways, had informal arrangements with a number of tourist operators in the region. Ralph Frid, of smoking fish fame, was a ten-year-old boy at the time and remembers the afternoon well. Arnold landed on the lake and taxied over to the dock at Mazinaw Inn. As it turned out, none of the guests wanted to take the sightseeing trip that afternoon. The three boys who had flown in with Arnold, Ken Kirk (the son of the resort operators on Big Gull Lake), Bob Butters of Toronto and Larry Chandler of Montreal, returned to the plane as it prepared to take off once more. The plane took a long taxi, eventually became airborne and was well above the treeline when, suddenly, something went terribly wrong. Ralph can remember seeing the plane turn back towards the lake, stall and fall into the water like a stone.

It was difficult to imagine that anyone could have survived. Within seconds, a number of boats from both shores converged on the location of the crash. Ralph's older brother Warren, and a guest at the Inn, Ben Parks, were among the first on the scene. The plane, having flipped over, was now partially submerged. Arnold Fleiler was able to make it to the surface unaided. Ken Kirk also was able to surface despite the fact that he had a broken leg. The other two boys were trapped. To his credit, Arnold was the one who dove down repeatedly to rescue them. The second boy, Larry Chandler, was unconscious with a huge gash across the side of his face. He was dragged into the boat where Ben Parks gave him artificial respiration and revived him. Bob Butters seemed, at the time, to be fine but was later to be diagnosed with a cracked vertebrae. The three were then rushed to the Mazinaw Inn where they awaited an ambulance to take them to Belleville. Later that same day, Ben Parks, the man who had resuscitated Larry Chandler, had a heart attack.

Incredibly, this story had a happy ending. The boys recovered in reasonably quick order, Ben Parks survived the coronary and went on to live many more productive years and Arnold Flieler bought himself another plane. By the next season, he was flying again. The wreckage of the plane was dragged up onto the beach, where it remained for the rest of the summer, an object of fascination for the kids who lived along the shore.

Such a fortunate outcome, however, was not to be a number of years later, when John Cassidy, a 69-year-old man from Arnprior was involved in the fatal crash of a single engine aircraft just outside of Cloyne on May 1, 1995.[2]

Bon Echo Provincial Park has had a significant impact on the lake attracting approximately 170,000 visitors per year. With over 500 campsites on 6,643 hectares or 16,408 acres of land, the Park is administered by a staff of three permanent, eleven part-time and 44 seasonal employees. The camping facilities for both drive-in and walk-in tenting, as well as for trailers, are very popular. With several beaches for swimming, a boat launch, picnic areas, a Visitors Centre, an amphitheatre and chaplaincy services, the Park is well-equipped to meet a range of interests.

Park staff are assisted by a volunteer association called the Friends of Bon Echo Park. This active group, dedicated to preserving the natural and cultural heritage of the Park, provides support in a variety of ways. They operate a gift shop and also publish a variety of trail guides. In 2000, the group hosted the fifth Bon Echo Art Exhibition and Sale, an exhibit of nature art by both local and other artists. Its members also volunteer to drive two sightseeing boats; the *Wanderer Too* and the *Mugwump*. The former craft provides an interpretive tour of the waters at the base of the cliff, while the latter is used to shuttle visitors over to the dock at the start of the Cliff Top Trail. The *Wanderer* was the name of the original boat which brought people up from the south end of the lake to Bon Echo Inn. The title *Mugwump* was borrowed from Merrill Denison, a name he used to describe himself – as being someone who had his mug on one side of the border and his

Entrance to Bon Echo Park. Courtesy John Campbell.

South Beach in mid-season. Courtesy John Campbell.

Canoe rentals provide easy access to the ancient rock face. Courtesy Astrid Fernandez.

The Wanderer Too *taking on passengers.* Courtesy John Campbell.

wump on the other, referring to his time spent living in Detroit and New York City as well as Canada, and to his dual citizenship.

Hiking is one of the Park's highlights and is available along a series of trails that vary in challenge from an interesting nature walk to a more ambitious hike. Trails include; the Shield, High Pines, Bon Echo Creek and the Cliff Top. For the more ambitious hiker there is also the Abes and Essens Trail. All three loops of this trail total a distance of 17 kilometres with each trail having a guide pamphlet which describes the flora and fauna characteristically found along the route. Park staff provide a large number of programs and events including interpretive nature hikes as well as evening programs. All activities are designed to support the Park's key values of recreation, education and conservation.

When the Park was first opened, many of the local cottagers were concerned that such use of the site would lead to increased pollution, traffic, noise and rowdy behavior. In reality, the Park has proven to be a good neighbour. While well-used, it is professionally supervised and kept in beautiful condition. Research also continues to be conducted on how this unique setting can be better understood, enjoyed and preserved.

On Labour Day, 1956, the first officially recorded climb of the face of Bon Echo was conducted by three members of the Toronto Alpine Club. A report from that same year in the *Napanee Beaver*, however, asserted, albeit somewhat lamely, that a successful climb had occurred much earlier in 1935:

*Along the Abes and Essens Trail
within the park.* Courtesy Ministry
of Natural Resources.

*Mr. Richmond, who now makes cheese in Dorland, was working on
the construction of Highway 41, which was being built at the time.
He and a fellow worker walked across the ice on a Sunday in early
winter, and climbed the face of the rock, with virtually no equipment,
according to the Beaver's informant. At the time of going to press, Mr.
Richmond was not available for comment on this report.*

While such a pursuit sounds exciting, unfortunately, three people
have died while attempting to climb on or near the rock face, one
in each of the years 1968, 1989 and 1995. One unfortunate young
man by the name of Matt Czech, was the last to meet this fate. Brad
Everson reported the story in the Sunday, September 24, 1995
edition of the *Ottawa Citizen*.

Matt was an experienced climber with five years of experience and
had traversed this particular spot on Bon Echo's face six times before.
On this day, however, something was to go terribly wrong. He was
climbing with a partner, Jean-Claude Neolet. They were part way up
the face when suddenly a piton gave way, and Matt and Jean-Claude
found themselves falling together towards the water below. It is esti-

mated that they hit the surface of the lake at approximately 120 kilometres per hour, still tethered together by a short length of nylon rope. They plunged down deep into the water to a depth where everything was completely dark. Neolet felt a sharp pain in his shoulder and back, but retained consciousness. Matt did not. Neolet struggled to swim and finally made it to the surface gasping for air. He struggled to the cliff edge where he obtained a hand-hold. The pair were still attached by the rope and Matt was now sinking, weighted down by his heavy climbing equipment. Jean-Claude tried desperately to pull Matt up with his one free hand but to no avail. He, himself was now in danger of being pulled down. Screaming for help, he managed to hold on until a pair of canoeists came to his assistance. They got him up on to a ledge where he could crouch.

More boats now arrived and others furiously pulled on the rope to bring Matt to the surface, but the rope was snagged. It would take several more agonizing minutes before he could be brought to the surface. By the time his body was recovered, it had been submerged for approximately 15 minutes and, while attempts were made at resuscitation, Matt was declared dead at Kingston General Hospital three hours after his fall. His partner Jean-Claude Neolet, had received a spinal fracture in the mishap and was to spend the next number of months recuperating in his home town of Terrebonne, Quebec.

The present stairs, on the south side of Bon Echo, provide a much safer alternative for visitors. Built in 1980, they were lifted in by helicopter.

During the late 1970s and 1980s, Northbrook gained notoriety as the hometown of David Trumble. This gentleman was touted as being Canada's oldest citizen, having been born in 1867, the same year as Confederation. The December 21, 1977 edition of the *Napanee Beaver* reported a number of the salient facts. Even in his later years, he was a tall, big-framed man with broad shoulders. He was married four times, fathered 19, and was grandfather to over 100. He received congratulations from Prime Minister Pierre Trudeau, was introduced to the Members of Parliament and appeared on the CBC program *Front Page Challenge*. During his life, he had been a

Rock climbing, an increasingly
frequent activity. Courtesy
Astrid Fernandez.

logger, miner, soldier and farmer. Trumble quit smoking at age 100,
and drinking at 104. When asked for the secret of his longevity, he
often mentioned his elixir of ginger root, brandy and oil from the
glands of a beaver. He claimed he could climb a tree backwards after
a shot of this concoction mixed with warm whiskey.

David Trumble also dictated two books when he was over 100,
the first selling over 7,000 copies. These books are filled with stories
of his adventures living in the rural Ontario of the time. A number
of these tales concerned the fights of his youth. One such skirmish
took place at a dance in Coe Hill:

> *Sure the whole seven of them came and they was going to give me a*
> *licking. So I just backed up into a corner and I said, OK boys, I'm*
> *ready for Coe Hill. There was two buildings together, you know, in*
> *a corner and they couldn't get by me and I had them there and I was*
> *just a kicking and a flailing. Well I knocked the whole seven of them*

Stairs provide for a safer trip up and down the Rock.
Courtesy Astrid Fernandez.

down just as fast as they could come at me. Then I grabbed my bottle of whiskey and my slippers and I went home.[3]

While Trumble was a warm-hearted and colourful story teller, unfortunately, after his death some doubt surfaced about his actual age.

Mazinaw Lake is located half way between Petawawa and Trenton. This seemingly insignificant fact means that it is a favourite rest point for members of Canada's Armed Forces who travel between the two centres. The March 24, 1982 edition of the *Napanee Beaver* tells of the winter's day that members of the Canadian Airborne Regiment dropped in for a cup of coffee at McKenzie's Restaurant which, over the years, had become a favourite place to stop. Flying out of Trenton at an altitude of 380 metres, the paratroopers jumped out of three Hercules aircraft over the upper lake. It was a spectacular sight to see the air filled with soldiers guiding their chutes to a safe landing on the ice. Once assembled at the restaurant, they finished off their exercise by presenting Jean McKenzie with a plaque in appreciation for the warm hospitality which they had received over the years.

Before the creation of the amalgamated municipality of North Frontenac in 1998, Barrie township had a population of 700, with an additional 2,575 seasonal residents. Today, farming has been replaced by other economic activity and plays a much less significant role in the life of the community. Exceptions, however, do exist. The Hook's 38 hectare, about 70 acres, pheasant farm near Flinton is one example. They ship internationally to gourmet restaurants and also supply game preserves, hunting clubs and hobby farmers.

The most significant types of employment include a range of enterprises: small business, construction, retail trade and government services (including transportation, natural resources, social services and education). The tourism industry, which Denison foresaw as the area's prime economic hope, has indeed flowered. His gift of the parkland has assisted in no small measure. As well, there is a growing population of retired residents who stay for most, if not all, of the year, thereby increasing the local market for goods and services.

Cloyne is the home of the North Addington Education Centre. This school was opened by the then Minister of Education, Robert Welch, in November of 1971 and was the first continuous school constructed in the province, offering education for children from Grade 1 to OAC. This meant that students, who at one time would have had to move away from home to attend secondary school, could now remain in their local community. The school's athletic program focuses on volleyball and, in 1984, their senior boys volleyball team was the Ontario Federation of Secondary School Athletic Association "A" Volleyball provincial champions, the first time the championship had been won by a school east of Toronto. Courses for adults are offered in the evening and opportunities for learning also are supported by the local library.

Health care is provided by the medical centre in Northbrook. Ambulance service is now available locally and a helicopter pad and airstrip, located in Northbrook, can be used in emergencies to transport patients to Kingston.

While local crime is not unheard of, it is often those who are passing through that grab the headlines. On December 20, 1990, the bank in Northbrook was robbed by armed bandits in broad daylight. The *Tweed News* gave this report:

> *According to a release from the Kaladar OPP, both suspects were wearing balaclavas and armed with sawed off shotguns. After holding up bank employees, the suspects were last seen south-bound on Highway 41 from Northbrook. An undisclosed amount of cash was taken and the investigation is continuing. . . . Paula Watson, manager of the Bank of Montreal for Tweed and Northbrook, said, "The customers and staff should be commended. They were all very calm and organized, and thankfully no one was injured." She also said that the community of Northbrook has been very supportive.*

Fortunately, the gunmen were captured shortly thereafter, and appropriately tried and sentenced.

Like most sparsely populated areas of the province, the people of this region often have to travel long distances to shop or avail themselves of government services. Frequently, emergencies have to be dealt with by those close at hand, with assistance from larger centres used as back-up support. Fire fighting provides a good example. While small fires are a periodic occurrence, on April 26, 1998, a large 80 hectare (200 acre) fire broke out west of Kaladar off Highway 7. The Kaladar/Barrie fire fighters successfully fought what could have been a disaster for the area, had it been allowed to get out of control. Reinforcements from Tweed and Sheffield assisted. A Provincial Government Beaver aircraft was also sent in to make more than a dozen water bombing passes over the fire. While this outside assistance was appreciated and needed, the local firefighters also were called out to fight a grass fire on property beside nearby Skootamatta Lake and a large house fire in Northbrook on the same weekend. These smaller incidences they took care of on their own.[4]

A sense of self-reliance in the local communities also is reflected in an impressive list of activities:

• The Chamber of Commerce and the local Lions Club are very active. Indeed, the Lions Club was instrumental in helping to raise funding for the building of the 60 bed Pine Meadow Nursing Home. The Lions also host a number of fund-raising events, the largest of these being the Blueberry Jamboree which has been held each Civic Holiday weekend for the past several years. This affair offers a pancake breakfast, baking contests, midway, dances and lots of musical entertainment. In 1997, it was featured on the CBC's "The National" news as an example of small town initiative.

• "Showcase 2000" is held in Cloyne each year in August. Started over a decade ago by people who had taken craft courses at the North Addington Education Centre, it now includes many outside exhibitors and is extremely well attended.

• The "Mazinaw Country Studio Tour" is an annual summer event featuring the works of local artists and woodcrafters.

• In September 1999, the fifth annual Snider's Open Golf Tournament was held at the local golf course.

• The start of the winter season is marked with the Kaladar Santa Claus parade.

• With the first several snowfalls, snowmobiling brings in a large number of visitors to ride trails, regularly groomed by the Mazinaw Power Line Snowmobile Club. These trails form part of a network of trails, allowing snowmobilers to go as far as Quebec to the east and Lake Simcoe to the west. Every year there is a special snowmobiling weekend held in Cloyne; often over 500 participants are entered.

• The Land O'Lakes Glee Club meets regularly in the Cloyne

United Church. They benefit the community by performing for seniors' groups and at other local gatherings.

• Those in the Cloyne area have worked hard to build a new local fire station run by a volunteer fire department. They have come to the rescue of many and the presence of the fire station has lowered insurance rates for all residents.

• A small museum in Cloyne is a good source of historical information and was founded by a local Pioneer Club which also published two books, *The Oxen and the Axe*, and *Unto These Hills*. In the mid 1970s, this group also was instrumental in hosting several Lumberman's Picnics. The most popular of these events was attended by Miss Canada.

These accomplishments are all evidence of local communities which are working hard to build better and more interesting lives for their citizens. The region has even entered cyberspace with its own home page on the Internet, being served by "Mazinaw On Line."

While there is much that is positive, the Mazinaw region continues to face economic constraints and ongoing social evolution. As the baby boom generation continues to age, many of those who have come to know the region as summer visitors will retire to the area, spending much, if not all of the year in the vicinity. Gradually, this will mean an increased demand for local services and a boost to the local economy. Many of these retirees will also bring valuable skills and a desire to contribute through volunteer activity. Long standing, year-round residents will, however, be called upon to share both the region and local decision-making with new arrivals; not always an easy thing to do. If this inevitable change is to work for everyone's benefit, it will require a focus on the common good from all concerned.

PHYSICAL AND NATURAL SETTING
OF THE MAZINAW

1.5 billion years ago	Grenville geological province formed as part of the Canadian Shield
1 billion years ago	Area covered by a sea having a bottom composed of sand, silt and lime
1,050 million years ago	Area subject to folding of the Earth's crust, creating large hills travelling in a northeasterly/southwesterly direction.
10,000 years ago	Last of 4 glacial periods ends, area covered by post-glacial Lake Champlain, as waters subside. The Mazinaw fault becomes spillway for glacial waters with an accumulation of significant gravel and sand deposits
9,000 years ago	Modern forest period begins

CHAPTER 9

Physical and Natural Setting of the Mazinaw

The physical and natural setting of the Mazinaw region has been drawing visitors for decades. Indeed, these characteristics comprise the context for its social evolution. While the great pine forests of yesterday will never return, today's mixed coniferous and deciduous trees, combined with dry rocky barrens and low-lying wetlands, provide a beautiful and varied ecosystem. The combination of clear water, glaciated rock and sandy terrain add to its appeal. The real attraction, however, is Bon Echo Rock. This 107 metre sheer cliff of pink granite drops into water, which is just as deep at its base. Created by a fault in the earth's crust, it has been subjected to the effects of four glacial periods and centuries of weathering, all of which have contributed to its current rugged beauty.

Approximately 335 metres above sea level, Mazinaw is the first lake of the Canadian Mississippi River chain. Over the course of the Mississippi's 193 kilometre length, its elevation drops a total of 323 metres. The river follows a southern course through Mazinaw, then turns, running directly east to its confluence with the Fall River near the village of Lanark. From this point on, the river flows in a northerly direction through the towns of Carleton Place, Almonte,

Bon Echo as seen through the pines. Courtesy Elizabeth Barrett.

Pakenham and Galetta, until it empties into the Ottawa River. The water level in the lake is controlled by the Mississippi Valley Conservation Authority to prevent flooding downstream. This control results in a fluctuation of 1.5 metres in the lake's water depth over the course of a year. Divided almost completely by a sandy peninsula across from the Rock, the lake gives an appearance of being two. The gap of only 4.6 metres (15 feet), called the Narrows, joins what is referred to as the upper and lower lakes.[1]

Mazinaw Lake Characteristics

ASPECT	MEASUREMENT
Elevation above sea level	335 metres (1,100 feet)
Length	13 kilometres (eight miles)
Average width	1.2 kilometres (.75 miles)
Drainage area	298 square kilometres (185 square miles)
Surface area	1,630 hectares (4,028 acres)

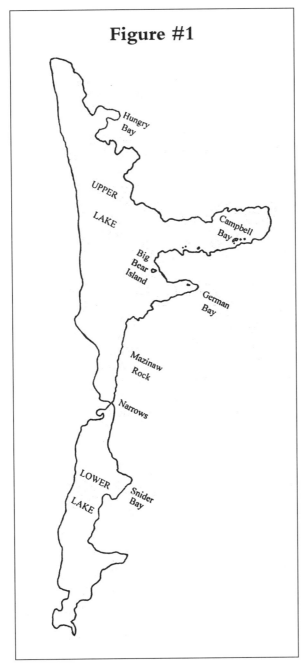

Figure #1

Mazinaw Lake. Developed by John Campbell from original map, Ministry of Natural Resources.

Figure #1 indicates the locations of the lake's bays and rivers. The lake is one of the deepest in the province. The upper lake is 137 metres (450 feet) at its deepest point, a zone which starts in the middle of the lake opposite the Rock and extends to an area across from the mouth of German Bay. In contrast, Campbell Bay, the largest bay, is quite shallow, being 12 metres (40 feet) at its deepest. This shallow depth is also a characteristic of the bay at the head of the lake. The lower lake has a maximum depth of 82 metres (268 feet). There is a small sand bar on the east side of the lower lake which averages approximately 1.8 metres in depth and was formed by the convergence of the current from Semicircle Creek joining with the main lake current coming down from the Narrows.[2]

Members of the Mazinaw Lake Cottagers' Association have volunteered their time to provide consistent water quality testing through the Ministry of Environment, Self Help Program since 1975. Comprehensive testing conducted by staff of the Mississippi Conservation Authority in 1998 provided for a comparison between water quality conditions now and those which existed in the 1970s. These results were published in the *State of the Lake Environment Report, December 1998: Mazinaw Lake.*

The findings indicate that water quality in the Mazinaw remains good. Water clarity, as measured by Secchi disk readings, has declined only marginally. Directly related to water clarity is the amount of nutrients entering the lake. There was a decrease in phosphorus from 9.0 micrograms per litre to 7.7. Any reading below 10 is considered to be acceptable. Chlorophyll, the green pigment found in algae, has decreased slightly since 1976. Levels average 1.5 micrograms/litre indicating an unenriched lake, conditions essential to sustain lake trout habitat.

Bacterial counts are well within acceptable limits although there are areas showing higher counts near cottages, storm sewers and the Park. Iron concentrations are normal except for elevated levels near the entrance of the creek from Semicircle Lake. The extremely low readings for algae, phosphorus and nitrogen also indicate that there is little nutrient enrichment.

The lake has a neutral pH. acidity level, typical of Precambrian Shield waterways. It is capable of withstanding heavy acidic buildup during spring run-off without biological damage. This is because of the large amounts of clay which underlie the rock and sand bottom and create a neutralizing influence.

Water temperatures vary according to season and depth. A study done on September 16, 1998 by the Mississippi Conservation Authority indicates that, at that time of year, surface temperatures are in the 18 C to 19 C range, with much colder temperatures of 8 C to 9 C at the 10 metre (30 foot) level. A definite levelling off of temperature occurs below this depth. While most visitors are not affected by such findings, fishermen who are intent on catching certain species, such as lake trout, and the scuba divers who sometimes can be seen diving in water near the cliff, must be aware of this significant temperature difference.

The future appearance and health of the lake is up to all of us. The municipal and provincial governments have important roles to play in preserving water quality and promoting appropriate land use through regulation and education. Those of us who are property owners, however, have a special responsibility that goes beyond legislated requirement. Collectively, we have a choice. Mazinaw can go the way of many other lakes in Southern Ontario, becoming little more than a suburban environment, or we can all take individual action to preserve and enhance the wilderness character of the lakescape. Voluntary strategies such as planting vegetation buffers between the lake and cottages or trailers, and ensuring that muted and natural colours are chosen for buildings can make a big difference. The Mississippi Valley Conservation Authority can assist property owners with suggestions regarding appropriate landscape design and species selection. In their information sheet *Naturalizing The Shoreline* they make the following point:

> *Although it is the scenic beauty of the waterfront that entices people to build a cottage on the edge of a lake, many landowners. . . . fill in wetlands or replace natural vegetation with manicured lawns. . . . The*

consequences of such urbanization can be extremely detrimental. . . .
Loss of natural vegetation can result in decreased water quality,
increased shoreline erosion, increased nutrients that promote weed and
algae growth, warming of shallow waters and destruction of wildlife
and aquatic habitats. The shallow water and the first 10 to 15 metres
of shoreline at the edge of the lake is known as the ribbon of life,
because 90% of all lake life is born, raised and fed there. This rich,
complex habitat supports plants, microorganisms, insects, amphibians,
birds, mammals and fish. Unnatural changes to the shoreline can
destroy this delicate balance of aquatic and shoreline ecosystems.

The Rideau Valley Conservation Authority in their publication,
On The Waterfront, New Waterfront Traditions In Eastern Ontario elab-
orates on this theme:

The shoreline plants act as a buffer against wind, wave, and ice
erosion. They modify destructive forces, help keep the soil undisturbed
and the water clean. . . . Every small rootlet takes a few more nutri-
ents out of the soil before they end up in the water. Every root hair
binds the soil together and helps prevent erosion. As a result, every
tree and shrub acts as a little environmental cleaning station with huge
benefits for the water quality of the lake.

Your lot is part of a well-connected ecosystem produced by ten
thousand years of natural evolution. . . . The trees, the rocks, the thin
soil, the ferns and flowers . . . are part of a bigger natural system that
supports water quality of the lake, preserves fish and wildlife habitat
and incidently increases the value and natural beauty of the shore.

Most people want a modest view of the lake from their cottage.
But clear cutting the natural vegetation is not necessary. Pruning
shoreline vegetation for a view is an attractive alternative. You keep
the shade and wind protection and add a nice view to the water. Avoid
removing good wildlife trees and shrubs like dogwood, cedar, aspen
and pine. Cut just the branches in your line of sight and leave the
rest.

The Mazinaw is a part of the Canadian Shield (a Precambrian bedrock which covers three quarters of the province). Specifically, Mazinaw Lake is located on a southerly spit of the Shield called the Frontenac Axis, which runs in a north/south direction through an area of much softer, younger sedimentary rock (limestone and shale) and richer soil called the St. Lawrence Lowlands. The Axis extends southward between the villages of Actinolite and Perth, forms the Thousand Islands and crosses into the United States, finally connecting with the Adirondack Mountains in Upper New York State.

Geologists who have studied the Canadian Shield have identified distinct areas called provinces which often have different characteristics and origins. These ancient land masses shifted and collided with one another. Bon Echo is part of the Grenville geological province which is the youngest of the Shield's provinces, being formed approximately one and a half billion years ago.

A billion years ago, the whole of Eastern Ontario was covered by a great sea having a bottom composed of sand, silt and lime. At this same time, there was considerable volcanic activity as lava and solid chunks of volcanic rock exploded from vents and fissures in the sea bottom, spreading volcanic rock over huge distances. This older volcanic rock makes up what is known as the Mazinaw Lake Metavolcanic Complex and the still older Tudor Metavolcanic Complex. There are rock outcroppings at the corner of Highways 506 and 41, between Northbrook and Cloyne, which are good examples of lava "pillows" dating from this period. These formations look like flattened ovals of rock and were formed by the original lava flow as the molten rock oozed out, much as toothpaste comes out of its container. These sites are relatively undamaged, having escaped the worse effects of glaciation.

The region was subjected to at least two periods during which folding of the earth's crust occurred, the most recent being about 1,050 million years ago. The folding was caused by large sections of the earth's crust being forced closer together by tremendous pressures as the Earth cooled. Large hills were produced in a northeasterly/southwesterly orientation. Heat and pressure from this activity modified both the sedimentary rock and lava flow into metamorphic rock. The once horizontal layers of rock were shoved up. Today these layers lie at a steep angle, dipping to the north and east. The folds consisted of layers of harder and softer rock. The softer rock experienced accelerated erosion and glacial gouging, thus creating many steep inclines and trenches. Some of the trenches filled with water and became lakes.

Just north of Northbrook, there is a narrow outcropping known as the Hastings conglomerates. This metamorphosed limestone has pebbles from an earlier age imbedded in it. It may be that this area was once an old river bottom, or the shore of an ancient lake. In any event, the pebbles can be clearly seen, trapped in the matrix of the surrounding rock. During the folding that occurred, many of the pebbles became elongated as the massive pressure squeezed the rock.

Quartz is white and glassy in appearance and veins of this rock can be discovered throughout the Mazinaw area. This mineral has a melting temperature of 900 degrees Celsius, far below that of many minerals. It is thought that the rock in this region may have been partially melted during its early history. The quartz, melting first, accumulated in cracks and crevices and then cooled. Veins of other elements, including precious metals, can be explained in a similar fashion.

The pink granite which forms the Bon Echo cliff, and underlies most of the immediate region, is called the Mazinaw Lake Pluton. It is the youngest rock in the area and was created during a period of active vulcanism. It is believed that a large opening, or magma chamber, was created by pressures within the earth. Molten lava, known as magma, flowed into this chamber, then cooled and crystallized forming what is known as a pluton. Over time, the rock covering the pluton was eroded, exposing the younger rock dome. A fault occurred, probably about one hundred million years ago, due to expansion or contraction of the earth's crust. An earthquake may have also been associated with this activity. Because of this movement, a zone of crushed debris was created along the fault line. This debris eroded away faster then the main mass of rock. It is the combination of these actions which resulted in the formation of Bon Echo.

The total Mazinaw area was subjected to considerable disruption. Bon Echo has several faults running in an east/west direction which divide its face into several sections. These smaller faults have formed into thickly forested valleys between sections of the cliff top. In addition, there is a crack in the top the Rock which parallels its face. The cliff also has large hollows in it below the water line and when the weather is very stormy, the water can produce a groaning sound.

The streaks of white on the Rock's face are calcium carbonate (lime) which has been dissolved by rainwater. When the water evaporates, the white residue remains. The dark bands, also in evidence, were formed after the rock solidified, when molten material of a different composition pushed into its cracks (maffick dikes). These bands all run at the same angle and are composed of a softer rock. The dikes have eroded faster than the surrounding rock, thus forming crevices.[3]

Until 10,000 years ago, glaciers covered the Mazinaw area. They came and retreated four times, were over one-and-a-half kilometres thick and exerted nine billion tons of pressure per square inch.

Glacial erratics. Courtesy Ministry of Natural Resources.

Under such conditions, the lower layers of the glacier became plastic-like in consistency and crept along, picking up debris and acting like sandpaper on what was beneath. Both glaciation and weathering have worked to soften the edges of Bon Echo. The glaciers approached from the northeast. Today, glacial grooves, and chatter marks (a series of small curved scars, usually convex, pointing towards the direction that the ice moved) can clearly be seen at the main lookout area on the top of the Rock.

With the retreat of glaciation, sediment was deposited in the form of sand hills and spillways, as well as clay and sand plains. These deposits were formed by residue from both glacial and post-glacial waters. The post-glacial Lake Champlain covered much of Eastern Ontario. During this period, the Mazinaw fault became a significant spillway for water melting from the glaciers. The peninsula which forms the Narrows, across from Bon Echo, is a spit created by sand and gravel deposits. Bon Echo Creek which was a larger river at that time, cut through this sand washing considerable debris into the lake helping to create the lagoon just to the south of the Narrows. There are a number of other locations in the immediate area where there is a thickness of 15 to 18 metres of sand and gravel sitting on the

Aerial view of the Rock, showing the Narrows. Courtesy Ministry of Natural Resources.

bedrock. Gravel deposits are located at both ends of the lake. Commercial gravel pits are located at the south end, in a geological formation known as the Cloyne Spillway. As one walks through the woods, every once in a while large boulders appear standing on their own. These boulders are called erratics and were deposited as the glaciers melted and retreated to the north.

Tillable soil is site specific, usually located on clay and sand flats. Even these soils, however, are generally coarse in texture, acidic and shallow. Only five percent of the land in the former Barrie township is classified as agricultural and even this land is considered marginal. None of the land in the former townships of Effingham, Anglesea, Abinger, Denbigh and Kaladar is considered agricultural. According to publications of the provincial Ministry of Agriculture and Rural Affairs, Mazinaw is in a large geographic area in which the soil averages 30 centimeters in thickness. This shallow soil explains the fallen trees, uprooted by storms, which one often encounters in the woods. These have been toppled by windstorms because the humus soil is so shallow, that the trees have not been able to put down deep root systems. The bedrock, like much of the Canadian Shield, is highly resistant to weathering and the terrain is relatively steep. Hence, much of the sediment produced by erosion and plant growth is carried away by water run off. Fire also has had its effect. Flames, which spread across much of the area in the latter part of the last century, often burned the soil to the underlying rock and left the soil exposed to erosion.

Despite these obstacles, a certain amount of replenishment has occurred. The Mazinaw area has many rock outcroppings and it is common to notice lichen growing on these rocks. Lichen, an essential soil builder, is actually made up of two plants – an algae and a fungus. The algae manufactures food for itself while the fungus absorbs moisture and provides a solid structure for the algae to live on. Neither could exist on its own. There are several different types of lichen: crestose have a hard crust; fruticose are tiny, shrub like in appearance and usually grow on soil or on decaying wood; foliose are leafy in appearance with crinkled edges. Lichen can withstand extremes of heat or cold by going into suspended animation. They reproduce by the releasing of spores which travel the wind and survive by producing sugar for food. A byproduct of this sugar production process is acid which helps to break down the rock on which they cling. Over time, the plant mass also provides humus, in which moss and grasses can grow. In this manner, soil is built up and enriched until suitable for other plants.

In the Mazinaw forest both bacteria and fungi are agents of regeneration. Fungus is not a true plant because it cannot produce food on its own. It is parasitic, living off dead plant material. If fungi were not doing their job, the forest would soon be choked in litter, leaves, fallen tree trunks and branches. The largest part of the fungus is the white thread–like filament which spreads through dead organic matter. Mushrooms and the white or orange masses which are often seen on the sides of decaying trees are its fruit.

The Mazinaw region is a part of the transition forest of the Southern Canadian Shield. In this type of forest, there are approximately 40 predominant tree species. The most common include red and white pine, maple, ash, beech, cedar, hemlock, spruce, balsam fir, birch, oak, and aspen. Tree species tend to clump together in areas to which they are specifically suited. Oak, like the pine, prefer open, rocky, dry places, often on the top of slopes. They are suitably adapted to these areas with their deep roots and waxy, scalloped leaves. The Mazinaw region represents the more northerly range for this species, being more characteristic of forests further to the south. What is commonly known in the area as poplar, is actually large tooth aspen. A related species called trembling aspen is also found. This latter species has a longer leaf stem which allows the leaf to tremble in the slightest breeze. Both aspen and birch need sun. They are transition trees, growing very quickly but having a relatively short life cycle. The aspen last approximately 90 years and the birch about 100 years. Throughout the Mazinaw region, acidic peat bogs occupy depressions in the bedrock. Cedar, balsam fir, tamarack (larch) and black spruce occupy these wetter, sunny areas. While no longer the predominant species, pine are common. White pine, with its soft feathered appearance, and red pine, characterized by its rough reddish bark and clumped needles, thrive in those areas around the lake which are sunny and have dry, sandy soil. These trees are very disease and insect resistant. The lower branches become shaded as the tree matures, however, and many die and drop off. Hemlock can be seen in the cool, forested areas. They like clay soils which hold the moisture. Because they are shade resistant, unlike the pine, their lower branches do not die. These trees catch almost all of the available sun with their dense branches and short flat needles. This means that there is little ground level growth in groves of hemlock. Deer are attracted to these groves in winter because the branches hold most of the snow.

Slowly, the Mazinaw forest is changing. The trees which now form the forest canopy are those which are adapted to open sunny environments and grew up after the fires: pine, oak, aspen and birch. Forty years ago, there were many more groves of young trees and the underbrush was denser. These trees are now mature. The second-tier trees are largely maple and beech. As the aspen and birch die off, they will be replaced by the more shade tolerant species. Many trees, especially the pine, find it difficult to compete with maple because it produces a thick ground cover with their large leaves. The small seeds of the pine find it hard to penetrate this barrier while the maples have large seeds and can root in such conditions. Eventually, it will be the beech and maple which will predominate, with hemlock and cedar growing in the swampier areas. Pine and the other species will continue to exist, but will not dominate. In many parts of Southern Ontario, maple constitutes 80 percent of the trees in the forest.

On some of the ridges and slopes surrounding Kiskebush Lake, there are stands of very old trees which were not disturbed by the loggers because of their inaccessibility. There are massive sugar maple, beech and yellow birch, some of which have tree trunk diameters of up to a metre. There are very few trees of this size and age left in Ontario.[4]

With so many maple and oak trees, the Mazinaw area is known for the brilliance of its fall colours. This region of eastern Ontario experiences a colder autumn than the area further south, adjacent to Lake Ontario. This fact, combined with a mixed forest of both coniferous and deciduous trees, makes for a truly spectacular setting for hiking or photography.

The cliff top of Bon Echo is a fragile habitat. The shallow soil is sandy and exceedingly thin. Baked by the sun, it is a dryer and hotter ecosystem than the surrounding forest. The plants which grow here need to be drought resistant. Predominant plants include red oak, white pine, junipers, serviceberries, low blueberry, sweet fern, sedges, poverty grass, hair grass, bristly sarsaparilla, bracken fern, whorled loosestrife and rusty woodsia. The most common tree on the cliff top is the red oak. Although between 65 and 90 years old, these trees are stunted because of the dry growing conditions and at full maturity may only reach 4.6 meters (fifteen feet) in height.

Low sweet blueberry bushes are a common ground cover. These plants also lead a fragile existence. While each plant can live for over 100 years, it is very difficult for seedlings to become established. Each berry contains 40 to 70 seeds, but most perish on the hot sandy soil. Those that do manage to germinate are usually killed by the frost. According to Park staff, the conditions for a seedling to survive are so specific that, for parts of Eastern Ontario, no new seedlings have established themselves for 60 years. Fortunately, they can also propagate by establishing new shoots from the root system of an existing plant.

The Park's Cliff Top Trail, with its two lookouts, provides an excellent view of the lake and surrounding countryside. This trail, however, cuts through this particularly dry and fragile ecosystem and, unfortunately, there is now evidence of damage from heavy traffic. Park staff have taken a number of steps to deal with this problem. Fencing has been erected to restrict access off the path and vegetation matting is being used to cover particularly eroded areas. The matting prevents further erosion, retains moisture and protects seeds during germination and early life. Wooden steps also have been installed along the path to slow and divert water run-off, thus reducing erosion. Even with these measures, damaged areas will take a considerable time to regenerate.

On the face of Bon Echo, there are cedars that obtain much of their

Left and below: View of the Upper Lake from Bon Echo. Courtesy John Campbell.

South shore framed in sumac and red oak. Courtesy John Campbell.

moisture and nutrients from the air. Some are as old as 1,000 years and are referred to as the Mazinaw Bonsai Cedars because of their gnarled and stunted appearance. This vegetation represents a rare example of old growth forest. The rock face was inaccessible and of no economic use and thus was not exploited. It is truly most beautiful and, while it looks rugged, great care must be taken for its preservation.

There are many rocky barren sites in the immediate vicinity. One such area, south of Kaladar on Highway 41, supports the growth of cactus (Opuntia fragilis). This is of particular significance because the nearest location known for this species to grow in the wild is in Wisconsin 1,000 kilometres (600 miles) to the west. The only other Canadian site is in the Lake of the Woods area, west of Thunder Bay. This local site is now protected by the Moira River Conservation Authority.

As one travels up Highway 37 from Belleville and Tweed, just after passing through the village of Actinolite, but before reaching Highway 7, the geography changes from sedimentary limestone to the igneous and metamorphic rock of the Canadian Shield. Driving further along Highway 7 to Kaladar and then north into Mazinaw country, one can see a number of low-laying bogs and wetlands in which a variety of vegetation flourishes.

Park visitors examining erosion damage on the Cliff Top Trail. Courtesy John Campbell.

The Mazinaw
"Bonzai Cedar."
Courtesy Lorna Seaman.

There is a spruce-larch bog formed in a kettle-hole lake located 1.2 kilometres (.75 of a mile) east-southeast of Abes Lake near the Park boundary. This lake fills a depression left by a large chunck of ice, which became dislodged and partially buried as the last glacier retreated. Usually associated with more northerly latitudes, this, and other bogs in the area, represent good examples of boreal vegetation within a transition forest landscape.

There are several small lakes that feed into Kilpecker Creek at the head of Mazinaw. Here a wide variety of wetlands vegetation can be observed. Some of the most common species include: water lilies, duckweed, cattails, burr reed, sedges, spike rush, eel grass, royal fern and pickerel weed. Semicircle Creek, which feeds into the southwest corner of the lake, and Bon Echo Creek, at the south edge of the Park, also support an interesting variety of wetlands vegetation. A common sight are a number of fern types, including the interrupted fern which grows about 50 centimetres (one and a half feet) high and is named for the large space in the leaflets at the top

*Entrance to Semi-
Circle Creek.*
Courtesy Astrid
Fernandez.

and bottom of the stem. The spaces contain spore bearing leaflets which wither and turn dark brown in the early summer.[5]

Most wild flowers require bright sunlight to thrive and thus grow in the open areas along the roads, or in meadows and abandoned fields. These plants are well adapted to the sunny, dry and sandy ecosystem which predominates. Daisies and black-eyed susans bloom in profusion in late June through to August. Other varieties include orange lilies, wild carrot (Queen Ann's lace), wild rose, thistle, touch-me-not, milkweed, Indian paintbrush, buttercups and gentian. In the earlier part of this century, when there were more meadows and fields in the area, it can be assumed at there were more wild flowers than exist at present. Those fields have now largely been reclaimed by a second growth of poplar, birch, pine and sumac. The species which do grow in the forest (such as mayflower, trillium, violet, lady slipper, jack-in-the-pulpit), flower in the early spring before tree foliage blocks out the sunlight.

Insects are a defining element of the Mazinaw ecosystem. The topography of the region is characterized by faulted bedrock, which has created uneven water drainage patterns. Glacial gouging also formed many small depressions in the rock which trap water. The combination of both fast-running and slow-moving water is perfect habitat for the breeding of a vast array of insects. Some common to the Mazinaw area which use surface tension to skim on top of the water include; the water strider, the water measurer and the whirling beetle. Less often noticed are the insects which live just under the

Early spring trilliums. Courtesy Lorna Seaman.

water's surface. Examples include; the backswimmer, diving beetles, giant water bugs and larva of the mosquito, black flies and dragon-flies. Those airborne insects which are the most annoying are, of course, the ones which enjoy the taste of human flesh – mosquitoes, black flies, horse flies and deer flies. Others less obnoxious and really quite interesting include a wide variety of moths, butterflies, drag-onflies, flying beetles, wasps, damselflies and mayflies.

This insect population is governed by nature's checks and bal-ances. Once in a while, however, a species is introduced which upsets this balance. The Gypsy Moth is one such species which did considerable damage to the forests of the Northeastern United States and parts of Eastern Canada. The *Napanee Beaver*, in its May 7, 1986 edition, described how the Ministry of Natural Resources built a small airport north of the Mazinaw, 25 kilometres north of Cloyne as part of an effort to combat the Gypsy Moth in this area. Thirty five planes were used for the spraying program. The government spent $350,000 to build the runway which was 150 metres wide and 900 metres long. About 1,700 cubic metres of fill was hauled for its construction. It was equipped with sleeping accommodation, bath-rooms, washing facilities and large mixing tanks, all of which are gone today. Bacterial spray was used to attack the moth at the larva stage. The program lasted for several years but was later discontin-ued because the damage done by the Gypsy Moth proved to be spo-radic in nature and its intensity did not warrant the cost. While this insect is still to be found in the area, experience indicates that trees on the Canadian Shield, which are used to a harsh environment, can withstand defoliation to a far greater degree than those which have been exposed to stresses less frequently.

The food chain of the region is characterized by insect eaters and those carnivores which feed on insect eaters. Birds such as killdeers, prairie warblers, phoebes, woodpeckers, swallows, ducks, and herons are common. Other animals which feed directly on insects include: fish, frogs, toads, bats, mice, chipmunks, turtles, snakes, salamanders and raccoons.

The Mazinaw area forms part of the borderland between Northern and Southern Ontario. It is unusual to find a Canadian Shield habitat so far south. For this reason, Mazinaw is home to both plants and animals which are usually found either to the north or south. Some northern birds and animals include the kingfisher, raven, timber wolf and snowy owl, while more southerly species include the turkey vulture, prairie warbler, five-lined skink and grey squirrel.

Different species of fish like different habitat. Fish which inhabit the deeper waters of the lake include; lake trout, whitefish and lake herring; while shallower water is home to sunfish, bass, perch, pike, and walleye. In spawning season, the female lake trout build up gravel mounds for hatcheries, 90 percent of which are in water less than a 1.5 metres in depth.

The spawning of lake trout has been the subject of much debate at Mazinaw. The traditional trout-spawning shoals, all of which are in the upper lake, are being exposed, after eggs have been laid, due to the lowering of the water level in the late fall. To protect these eggs, the water level should be lowered by the first week of October, thus encouraging the trout to lay their eggs further out from shore. Studies have indicated that the native lake trout are far hardier than fingerlings raised in fish hatcheries, and that, if the lake level was lowered at the appropriate time, the natural trout population would thrive. There is opposition, however, from many of the cottagers with water access only, to any change in the date at which the water level is lowered. They want to have access until freeze up, or at least until after deer hunting season. This, of course, is not the first time that there has been debate over how the resources of the region should be managed.

The Conservationists of Frontenac and Addington is a hunting and fishing based organization which assisted in trying to find a solution. In addition to being involved in the management of a small fish hatchery, they assisted a project of the Mississippi Conservation Authority to move 77 cubic metres of rock into Campbell Bay to help rehabilitate lake trout spawning grounds. The rock was spread adjacent to traditional spawning grounds, but in deeper water. It was hoped that this effort would encourage the lake trout to spawn in an area left unaffected by the raising and lowering of the water level. Unfortunately, evidence, to date, does not indicate success. The spawning season for bass and walleye is in June and is not affected by water lowering. Lake trout spawn in October, however, and thus are vulnerable.

Testing of fish in Mazinaw indicates high levels of mercury, particularly in fish-eating species such as lake trout and walleye. There are eating restrictions on walleye over 35 centimetres (14 inches) and no lake trout over 54 centimetres (22 inches) should be consumed. It is the view of the Ministry of Natural Resources that the mercury contamination comes from natural bed rock and gravel sources, rather than from air pollution.[6]

Park staff have identified over 186 kinds of birds. Some of these species only visit during times of migration, the most exotic of these seasonal visitors being the majestic whistling swan. Many of the lake's feathered inhabitants are carnivores. Those commonly seen include: killdeers, phoebes, woodpeckers, swallows, owls, hawks, turkey vultures, kingfishers, ravens, swallows and heron. These birds provide a rich variety of appearance and behavior according to species.[7]

Turkey vultures are recent immigrants to the Mazinaw area. They have two-toned, black wings which form a shallow "V" shape, as they circle in the sky searching for food. Their wing span can grow up to 1.5 metes (five feet). This bird is a carrion feeder and has a keen sense of both sight and smell which it uses to locate the bodies of dead creatures from high above. On the ground they are very clumsy, moving with a cumbersome gait. To get airborne they often hop and leap around several times. Once airborne, however, this much maligned bird is one of the most graceful of the birds of prey. Because of its lighter bone structure, it can surf the air thermals even in light updrafts. Turkey vultures mate from mid April to May and do not construct a nest, but lay their eggs in a concealed spot. These same birds come back to the Mazinaw year after year. Of unusual appearance, these birds have red heads and necks with no feathers on them, which means they can feast on carrion without getting their feathers sticky. It also means, however, that their ability to handle cold weather is diminished. Bon Echo is near the northern edge of their summer feeding territory and like other birds of prey, they travel south for the winter.

Rarely sighted is the osprey, a fishing bird, a dive-bomber with talons that preys on fish almost exclusively. Their underside is white and they have a wing span up to 1 metre (3 feet). Ospreys nest in tall trees and mate for life. They lay two or three eggs and the chicks are brooded by the female. Chicks are able to take their first flight when eight weeks old.

One of the projects undertaken in the Park was an attempt to introduce the Peregrine falcon. The translation of the Latin word "Peregrine" means wanderer. In the summer of 1996, the last set of 12 falcon chicks were introduced. These were the offspring of parents who had been raised in captivity. Great care was taken to keep contact with humans to a minimum. This was part of a larger effort to introduce the Peregrines back into the province and was not site specific. In that sense it was successful but in the summer of 1997, only one lone Peregrine returned to Bon Echo. Similar results occurred with several other groups attempting to introduce this species in Eastern Ontario wilderness settings. The Peregrine, however, seem to have adapted to city life. There are now several nesting pairs in Toronto, living on the roof tops of tall buildings, high above the traffic, dive-bombing the pigeons.

Merganser ducks are primarily carnivores while mallards are plant eaters. That may explain why there are families of mergansers at Mazinaw but not mallards. The latter prefer lakes with mud bottoms and more water plants. Mergansers are diving ducks and eat cray-fish, frogs, and insects, as well as fish. With spike-like beaks with toothed margins the mergansers are well equipped for catching their prey. To get airborne, they have to take a greater run than do non-diving ducks, because their bodies are heavier. Mergansers remain on the lake until December freeze up.

The Loon and its haunting call are a true symbol of the wild places. The lineage of this ancient species can be traced back to pre-historic times. Like the mergansers, the loon is a fish- eating bird. Its legs are placed well back, it has a heavier body mass, large webbed feet and a stout, spear-like bill; all adaptations for diving and hunting fish. They can dive as far as 60 metres (two hundred feet) down and can stay underwater for up to five minutes. On land they are very awkward, shoving themselves along on their bellies with their feet. Loons lack natural enemies, but gulls, crows and small shore animals will eat their eggs from the nests which are located close to the shore. While loons prefer seclusion, they have adapted to the increased traffic and continue to nest in various reed beds located around the lake.

Along the banks of Bon Echo Creek there is a dirt bluff carved out by the creek. Norther rough-winged swallows and kingfishers use their claws to dig holes for nesting where the steep bank pro-vides protection against predators. Swallows also build nests in crevasses on the face of Bon Echo and are a common sight in the evening, swooping near the surface of the water hunting insects.

The Prairie warbler is rare in this part of the country, usually being found further south. It uses Bon Echo as a summer nesting site. This species likes to nest in juniper bushes and sits in small trees, not too high off the ground. It is an insect-eating little bird, which is not found in the prairies at all but is scattered across the eastern United States. The warbler has a small thin bill and a yellow face, dis-sected with two black lines which look like spectacles, and a yellow edged belly with black stripes. Its back is a yellowish-green and it has a black cap on its head. The female has the same markings, but is duller in colour. The song of the warbler is like a bottle being filled with liquid, going higher in pitch as the song continues.

Ravens are a bird more frequently observed in Northern Ontario, but are common here because of the Canadian Shield environment. Ravens can be distinguished from crows by their larger size, croaking instead of cawing, and wedged-shaped rather than square tails. At Bon Echo, ravens are more common than crows. Sometimes, like swallows, they nest directly on the cliff face.

There are at least 46 species of animals to be found in the Provincial Park. The only endangered, or rare, one is the long tail weasel. Species prefer habitat according to their means of locomotion and source of food. Appendix I details groupings of animals according to their preference for proximity to; lakes and rivers, wooded areas, and more mixed or open terrain.[8]

The small fur bearing animals, including the muskrat, mink, otter, fisher, marten, ermine and beaver, have made a comeback numerically in the Mazinaw area, despite the fact that trapping is still an active pursuit. According to the local trapping association, beaver pelts contribute approximately $750,000 to the local economy.

Deer are actually more common in areas to the south where there are more meadow lands and smaller trees and bushes to provide better foraging. In the off season Dear are a common sight in the Park and are plentiful north of Abes Lake where there is an extensive range with a winter population of close to 2,000 animals. Within this area, there has been an extensive deer improvement program to make up for the lack of natural browsing material. This project included the planting of large amounts of clover and was sponsored by the Conservationists of Frontenac and Addington. The adult whitetail deer only grows to a height of 1.2 metres (four feet) at the shoulders and weighs approximately 100 kilograms (200 pounds). They usually live for four to five years and travel in small groups. As the deer population is encouraged to grow, it is likely that a corresponding increase in the small local wolf population will follow.

Porcupines are found in wooded areas, preferring forests with a good mixture of aspen and pine and thus can be found in this area. Their numbers, however, have decreased in recent years. This may

The common loon. Courtesy Ministry of Natural Resources.

be due to the corresponding increase in the fisher population. Only the fisher and bobcat hunt porcupines.

Due to the large number of insects, a variety of amphibians are also common. Various species of frogs, toads, snakes and salamanders can be found. Mazinaw is also home to Ontario's only lizard, the five-lined skink, blackish brown in color, with five white or yellow stripes. This lizard is sighted most often in the Eastern and Southern United States. They like warm areas with lots of sun and thus find open areas, like Bon Echo, most attractive.[9]

This wide variety of flora and fauna lives in a delicate balance. The more we can understand and appreciate the tolerances of the various species and the nature of their inter-relationships, the more successful we will be in preserving the region's ecologic health and diversity. Much, of a motherhood nature, has been written about the importance of being environmentally aware. It will remain a challenge, however, to reflect the values of conservation and preservation in action as the area grows in popularity. The Mazinaw region needs protection from the dangers of water pollution, overuse and lakeshore exfoliation.

Epilogue

The Mazinaw story is a reflection of man's experience in a beautiful, rugged and challenging region of the Province: a Canadian Shield environment in a remote section of Southeastern Ontario.

While little, in terms of specifics, is documented about the experience of Aboriginal people in the immediate area, it is known that for centuries, small family bands visited on their seasonal sojourns, camping at the Narrows. We also know that the Rock was well known to the Native population and played a pivotal role in their relationship with the lake. The pictographs represent a nomadic, hunting and gathering society's attempt to make a connection with the spiritual world. They believed that Nanabush turned himself into Bon Echo, as well as other unique forms of nature, to help teach man to live with strength, kindness, courage and ingenuity. The Rock is a reflection of the elemental and eternal and, as such, is evocative, speaking to those who will listen. Down through the years, many have felt its spiritual presence.

Today, only an echo of the old logging days remain. A reminder that short-term economic gain should never be used as a substitute for long-term sustainability.

The experience of settlement in the region was one of economic struggle as families challenged a rugged and agriculturally unsuitable land to create a livelihood. It wasn't until the 1940s, that the region finally became an integrated part of Southern Ontario. It had taken 85 years, since the first settlers homesteaded along the Addington Road in 1855, to move from a condition of remoteness and inaccessibility. It would take another ten years, however, before tourism reached its potential as the engine of the local economy.

Of significant influence have been those associated with the original Bon Echo Inn; its founder Weston Price, an energetic young dentist and naturalist, Flora MacDonald Denison and her son Merrill under whose guidance the Inn became a centre for those interested in the arts and the poetry of Walt Whitman. The values they espoused stressed appreciation of nature and the esthetic, conservation, spiritual growth and equality.

The social context of the region has gradually evolved. The area's popularity with summer visitors has increased and local communities, long self-reliant, are continuing to actively pursue greater opportunities for their citizens.

The Mazinaw remains a priceless natural setting, a remote corner of Southeastern Ontario which is still largely unspoiled but which needs our protection. The region's mixed coniferous and deciduous trees, combined with rocky barrens and low wetlands, provide a beautiful and varied ecosystem. The combination of clear water, glaciated rock and sandy terrain add to its appeal. While wild and rugged in appearance, the lake, its shoreline and the broader region can be easily marred. This physical setting is also home to a wide variety of vulnerable plants and animals which must live in a delicately balanced interrelationship.

This then is the Mazinaw experience. Over the years, it has played a valued part in the lives of the many who have spent time by her shores. If this same unspoiled opportunity is to be available for future generations, we all must take both individual and collective responsibility for promoting conservation, preservation and appropriate stewardship.

Appendix 1

Creatures Common in the Mazinaw Area

Preferred Habitat	Species of Animal
Close to Lakes and Rivers	muskrat; beaver; raccoon; mink; otter; fisher; marten; weasel; ermine; snapping, Blandings and painted turtles; salamanders; northern water snakes; northern leopard frogs as well as American toads; mink and bull frogs.
Wooded Areas	spring peepers, grey tree frogs and wood frogs; chipmunks; red squirrels; porcupine; coyotes and grey wolves; black bears; lynx and bobcats.
Mixed Wooded and Open	white-tailed deer; red fox; coyotes; bats; rabbits; grey squirrels; white footed and deer mice as well as grey and wood land jumping mice; skunks; eastern garter snakes, smooth green snakes and milk snakes.

Appendix 11

Weather

Average temperature	5.6 C, (42 F)
January average temperature	-10 C, (14 F)
July average temperature	20 C, (68 F)
Frost-free days	130
Last frost	3rd week of May
First frost	4th week of September
Annual precipitation	80 cm (32 in)
average annual snowfall	175 cm (70 in)
precipitation in growing season (May to September)	35 cm (14 in)
Days with measurable precipitation	144 days

Endnotes

Chapter 1 : First Nations Period

1. Gene Brown, Nadine Brumell & Elsie Snider, (eds), *The Oxen And The Axe*. (Cloyne Ont.: The Pioneer Club of Cloyne, undated) 12.

2. Frank B. Edwards, *The Smiling Wilderness, An Illustrated History of Lennox and Addington County*. (Camden, Ont.: Camden House, 1984) 13.

3. ___, "Mississippi Valley Conservation Report History." (Toronto: Department of Energy and Resource Management, Queen's Printer, 1970) 1- 7.

Chapter 2 : Pictographs and Mythology

1. ___, *The Trail of Nanabush* (Toronto: Ministry of Natural Resources; Queen's Printer, 1984) not paginated.

2. *Tweed News*, June 21, 1967.

3. Robert Stacey and Stan McMullin, *Massanoga, The Art of Bon Echo*. (Ottawa: Penumba Press, 1998) 96.

4. Grace Rajnovich, *Reading Rock Art: Interpreting the Indian Rock Paintings of the Canadian Shield*. (Toronto: Natural Heritage/Natural History Inc. 1994) 161.

5. ___, *The Trail of Nanabush*.

6. Ibid.

7. Merrill Denison, Unpublished papers on the history of the Mazinaw area. (Bon Echo Provincial Park, undated).

8. Ibid.

Chapter 3 : Lumbering of the Mighty Pine

1. Brown, Brumell and Snider, *The Oxen and the Axe*. 27.

2. ___, "Mississippi Valley Conservation Report History." (Department of Energy and Resource Management, Queens Printer, 1970) 27.

3. ___, Gillies Brothers Lumber Company Papers. September, 1877. Agreement of Employment, Archives of Ontario F150-12-1-11.

4. Brown, Brumell and Snider, *The Oxen and The Axe*. 60 .

5. Byron Rollason (Ed.), *Country of a Thousand Lakes, The History of the County of Frontenac 1673-1973*. (Kingston, Ont.: Kingston-Frontenac County Council, 1982) 369.

6. ___ Gillies Bros, 1890. Bills for Supplies Ordered for the Shanties, Archives of Ontario F150 -12-1-11.

7. Wilfred Lessard, *The Village On The Skoot*. (Flinton, Ont.: Golden Circle Club, 1979) 20.

8. ___ "Mississippi Valley Conservation Report, History," 16

Chapter 4 : Settlement Along the Colonization Roads

1. Ebenezer Perry, "Report on the Addington Road for 1864." Archives of Ontario 34764-34765.

2. Ibid.

3. C.B. Cornell, Letter to Ebenezer Perry 1857. Archives of Ontario 34765 (F1166) (MS 702-R21)

4. Brown, Brumell and Snider, *The Oxen and The Axe*. 29.

5. Ebenezer Perry, "Report on the Addington Road for 1855." (Lennox and Addington Historical Society)

6. Ebenezer Perry, "Report on the Addington Road for 1863 and 1864." (Lennox and Addington Historical Society)

7. ___ "Bon Echo Provincial Park Facilities and Programs."(Toronto, Ont. Ministry of Natural Resources, Queens Printer: 1995) 10.

8. Samuel Lane, June /October, 1876, "Overseer's Road Construction Diaries, Addington Road, Colonization Roads Branch Ontario Government." Archives of Ontario RG52-V1-0-9 Box 1.

9. Brown, Brumell and Snider. *The Oxen and The Axe* . 28.

10. Lessard. *The Village On The Skoot*. 42.

11. ___ "Bon Echo Provincial Park Facilities and Programs, 1995." 3.

12. Lessard. *The Village On The Skoot*. 99.

13. Paul Stein, *A History of the Back End of Addington County*. (unpublished. Denbigh, Ont.: February 8, 1910); Archives of Ontario F1166, 30109.

14. Ibid (not paginated).

Chapter 5 : Continuing Settlement

1. Jane Weese, unpublished letter, (1954): Pioneer Museum, Cloyne, Ontario.

2. Interview with Ted Snider, July, 1998.

3. "Bylaw No. 1," March 4, 1899, Municipal Corporation of Kaladar, Angesea and Effingham, Archives of Ontario F1166, 32559.

4. Colonization Roads 1912, Petitions, Archives of Ontario RG52, Series 2A, Box 6.

5. Ron Brown, *Ghost Towns of Ontario*. (Lanley, Ont.: Stagecoach Publishing Co., 1978) 137.

Chapter 6 : Mining: An Unfulfilled Hope

1. Much of the information on mining in the Mazinaw area was found in the records of the *Tweed News*.

Chapter 7 : Bon Echo Inn – The Prices and the Denisons

1. Merrill Denison, unpublished papers on the history of the Mazinaw area, Bon Echo Provincial Park.

2. Ibid.

3. Merrill Denison, personal papers, 1933, Queen's University Archives, Kingston, Ont., Box 83 "Bon Echo".

4. Flora MacDonald Denison, personal papers, Thomas Fisher Rare Book Library, University of Toronto, Toronto Ont.

5. Merrill Denison, personal papers, 1933, Queen's University Archives, Kingston Ont., Box 83 "Bon Echo."

6. Ibid.

7. Stuart Mackinnon, *Mazinaw*. (Toronto Ont.: McClelland and Stewart, 1980) 57.

8. Savigny, Mary, *Bon Echo, the Denison Years*. (Toronto Ont.: Natural Heritage Books., 1997) 23.

9. Denison, Merrill, *Toronto Star Weekly*, Feb. 19, 1927

10. Merrill Denison, personal papers, 1933.Queens University Archives, Kingston Ont., Box 33.

11. Ibid.

12. Savigny,*Bon Echo, the Denison Years*. 35.

13. Ibid, 3,6,13.

14. Ibid, 4.

15. Ibid,11.

Chapter 8 : Recent History and the Growth of Tourism

1. "Camp Mazinaw," words by Doug Tisdall, tune by Finlandia Sibeluis, 1951.

2. *Toronto Sun*, May 2,1995.

3. *Napanee Beaver*, December 21, 1977.

4. *Ottawa Citizen*, July 14, 1995, C1.

Chapter 9 : Physical and Natural Setting of the Mazinaw

1. __ "The Mississippi River Watershed, Watershed Fact Sheet." Mississippi Valley Conservation Authority, P.O. Box 268 Lanark, Ont., 1997.

2. "Water Depth Profile," Ministry of Natural Resources, Queen's Printer, 1976.

3. "Cliff Top Trail." Bon Echo Provincial Park, Friends of Bon Echo, P.O. Box 229 Cloyne, Ontario. 14.

4. "Kishebus Canoe Trail." Bon Echo Provincial Park, Friends of Bon Echo Park in cooperation with the Ministry of Natural Resources, P.C. Box 229 Cloyne, Ontario.

5. __ "Bon Echo Provincial Park Facilities and Programs, 1995." 11.

6. "Mazinaw Lake Dam Environmental Study Report." Mississippi Valley Conservation Authority, (Lanark, Ont.: Ecos Garatech Consulting Engineers, May 1991).

7. "Bird Checklist." Bon Echo Provincial Park, Ministry of Natural Resources, Friends of Bon Echo, 1992.

8. "Mammal Checklist." Bon Echo Provincial Park, Ministry of Natural Resources, Cloyne, Ont.

9. __ "Bon Echo Provincial Park Facilities and Programs, 1995," 11.

Index

Pine and fern. Courtesy Ministry of Natural Resources.

Bibliography

__, "Bird Checklist, Bon Echo Provincial Park, Ministry of Natural Resources,"Cloyne Ont., Friends of Bon Echo, 1992.

__, "Bon Echo Provincial Park Management Plan, Ministry of Natural Resources,."Toronto, Ont.: Queen's Printer, 1991.

__, "Bon Echo Provincial Park, Facilities and Programs, Ministry of Natural Resources." Toronto, Ont.: Queen's Printer, years 1986 through to 1996.

Ron Brown,*Ghost Towns of Ontario.* (Langley Ont.: Stagecoach Publishing Co.) 1979

__, Bylaw No. 1, Municipal Corporation of Kaladar, Angesea and Effingham, March 4, 1899, Archives of Ontario, F1166, 32559

Nadine Brumell, Gene Brown, & Elsie Snider, (eds), *The Oxen And The Axe.* (Cloyne Ont.: The Pioneer Club of Cloyne). undated.

__, "Canoe Hike and Pictograph Tour," Bon Echo Provincial Park, Ministry of Natural Resources, Cloyne Ont.

__, "Cliff Top Trail," Bon Echo Provincial Park, Friends of Bon Echo, P.O. Box 229 Cloyne, Ontario

Alan M. Cvancara, *At The Water's Edge, Nature Study in Lakes, Streams and Ponds.* New York and Toronto. John Wiley & sons, 1989.

Gerald Durrell, *A Practical Guide For The Amateur Naturalist.* New York: Alfred Knopt, 1983.

Frank B., Edwards, *The Smiling Wilderness, An Illustrated History of Lennox and Addington County.* Camden Ont.: Camden House, 1984

Hilda Geddes, *The Canadian Mississippi River.* Burnstown, Ont.: General Store Publishing House, 1992.

J.E. Glen and Catherine Wills, "Our Vision In Focus, The Human Services Planning Exercise For Frontenac County, Final Report," Kingston Ont.:Kingston and Area Social Planning Council, March 1995.

Wilfred Lessard, *The Village On The Skoot.* Flinton Ont.: Golden Circle Club,1979.

Kit and George Harrison, *America's Favourite Backyard Wildlife.* New York: Simon and Schuster, 1985.

Joan Holmes, "Interpretation of the Archaeology of Bon Echo Provincial Park," Ministry of Natural Resources, Queens Printer (not dated).

Selwyn Dewdney and Kenneth Kidd, *Indian Rock Paintings Of The Great Lakes.* Toronto: Ont.:University of Toronto Press

___, "Kishebus Canoe Trail,"Bon Echo Provincial Park, Friends of Bon Echo Park in cooperation with the Ministry of Natural Resources, Cloyne, Ontario.

Wilford Lessard, "The History of Flinton," Bon Echo Provincial Park, Ministry of Natural Resources, unpublished manuscript, 1971.

___, "Life Science Areas of Natural and Scientific Interest in Site District 5-11," Ministry of Natural Resources, Eastern Region, Kemptville, 1990.

D. Macdonald, *The Mugwump Canadian, The Merrill Denison Story.* Montreal Quebec, Content Publishing Ltd., 1973.

Stuart Mackinnon, *Mazinaw.* Toronto: McClelland and Stewart, 1980.

___, "Mammal Checklist," Bon Echo Provincial Park, Ministry of Natural Resources, Cloyne, Ont.

___, "Mazinaw Lake Dam Environmental Study Report," Mississippi Valley Conservation Authority, Ecos Garatech Consulting Engineers, MVCA P.O. Box 268, Lanark, Ont. KOG 1KO, May 1991.

___, "Mazinaw Area," Bancroft District Office, Ministry of Natural Resources, 1993.

___, "Mississippi Valley Conservation Report History," Department of Energy and Resource Management, Queen's Printer, 1970.

___, "Mississippi Valley Conservation Report Volume 1," Department of Energy and Resources Management, Queen's Printer, 1970.

Napanee Beaver, March 9, 1994.

___, "Naturalizing The Shoreline," Mississippi Valley Conservation. Lanark, Ont. (undated)

Todd Norris, "A Life Science Inventory Of The Mazinaw Rock Clifftop; Bon Echo Provincial Park," Ontario Ministry Of Natural Resources, Tweed District, 1995.

___, "Reptile and Amphibian Checklist," Bon Echo Provincial Park, Ministry of Natural Resources, Cloyne, Ont.; Queen's Printer.

___, *Rocks and Minerals for the Collector.* Geological Survey of Canada, Dept. of Energy, Mines and Resources, Ottawa Ont.: Queens Printer, 1975.

Grace Rajnovich, *Reading Rock Art: Interpreting the Indian Rock Paintings of the Canadian Shield.* Toronto: Natural Heritage/Natural History Inc. 1994.

Bryan Rollason, ed., *County of a Thousand Lakes, The History of the County of Frontenac, 1673-1973.* Kingston, Ont.: Kingston Frontenac County Council, 1982.

Mary Savigny, *Bon Echo, the Denison Years.* Toronto Ont.: Natural Heritage Natural History Inc., 1997.

___, "Soil Associations of Southern Ontario," Ministry of Agriculture, Food and Rural Affairs, Queen's Printer.

Lake," Mississippi Valley Conservation Authority, Box 268, Lanark, Ont., 1998.

Paul Stein, "A History of the Back End of Addington County." Denbigh, February 8, 1910, unpublished, Archives of Ontario, F1166, 30109.

Ann and Myron Sutton, *The Audubon Society Nature Guides, Eastern Forests.* New York, Alfred Knopt, 1988.

___, *The North Of Seven Clarion – The Voice from RR#1, Arden, Ardoch, Cloyne, Denbigh, Flinton, Kaladar and Northbrook.* 1997.

___, "The Shield Trail," Bon Echo Provincial Park, Friends of Bon Echo Park, in cooperation with Ministry of Natural Resources, P.O. Box 229 Cloyne, Ontario, KOH IKO.

___, "Trail of Nanabush," Petroglyphs Provincial Park, Ministry of Natural Resources, Queen's Printer.

___, *Unto These Hills,* The Pioneer Club, Cloyne, Ont., 1978.

___, "Water Depth Profile," Ministry of Natural Resources, Queen's Printer.

Jane Weese, unpublished letter, Pioneer Museum, Cloyne Ont., 1954.

___, "1991 Socio-Demographic Profile for Frontenac and Lennox & Addington Counties Volumes 1&2." Kingston, Frontenac and Lennox & Addington District Health Council, 1994.

Rosemary Campbell

About the Author

John Campbell and his family have spent a part of each of the last 50 summers at their summer cottage on the lower lake at Mazinaw. He and his wife Rosemary have two children, Brian and Meghan, both now in their early twenties. Formerly employed by the Ontario Provincial Government in Toronto, John is currently a management consultant in the private sector. He is looking forward to spending more time at the Mazinaw as his work schedule permits; an opportunity to join three sets of aunts and uncles who have permanent residences on the Lake.

White water lily. Courtesy Ministry of Natural Resources.